The Shawshank Redemption

Mark Kermode

Publishing

First published in 2003 by the
British Film Institute
21 Stephen Street, London W1T 1LN

The British Film Institute promotes greater
understanding and appreciation of,
and access to, film and moving image
culture in the UK.

British Library Cataloguing-in-Publication Data
A catalogue record for this book is available
from the British Library

ISBN 0-85170-968-0

Series design by Andrew Barron
& Collis Clements Associates

Typeset in Italian Garamond
and Swiss 721BT by
D R Bungay Associates,
Burghfield, Berks

Printed in Great Britain by
Cromwell Press, Trowbridge, Wiltshire

Contents

Acknowledgments

Much of the groundwork for this book was laid by film-maker Andrew Abbott, director of the Channel Four documentary *Shawshank: The Redeeming Feature*. Quotations from this documentary are from interviews conducted largely by Andrew, occasionally by me, and (in the case of Frank Darabont) by David J. Schow. Quotations from Tim Robbins are from a FilmFour *Viewfinder* interview conducted by me. David J. Schow and Frank Darabont kindly made available an invaluable selection of production stills, which Nathan Long scanned. All stills are copyright © Castle Rock Entertainment, 1994. Production stills photographed by Michael Weinstein, except as noted.

With thanks, as ever, to Linda Ruth Williams.

FOR GEORGIA GRACE AND GABRIEL MICHAEL WILLIAMS

Prologue: A Redeeming Feature

I understand you're a man that knows how to get things ...
Andy Dufresne to Ellis Boyd 'Red' Redding

Unlike Red, I'm a man who doesn't get things. And one of the things I didn't get – at least initially – was *The Shawshank Redemption*. Not that I didn't think it was a good movie, impressively constructed, with an almost anachronistically efficient sense of good storytelling. But like most of the critics who reviewed *The Shawshank Redemption* when it was first released in 1994, I had no sense whatsoever that it would become many people's *favourite* movie; that it would be voted best film of the 1990s and fourth-best film *ever* by readers of *Empire* magazine; that it would rival *The Godfather* and *Star Wars* for the top spot of the Internet Movie Database subscribers' poll; that it would be quoted on national television by Sarah Ferguson, the Duchess of York, who had endured tough times.

Today, *The Shawshank Redemption* sits alongside such perennial favourites as *Casablanca* and *It's a Wonderful Life* in the pantheon of

Frank Darabont and Morgan Freeman on location at Mansfield Reformatory

'feel-good' cinema, an unlikely achievement for a low-key prison drama that failed to set the box office alight when it first opened, which garnered nominations rather than statuettes at the Academy Awards ceremony, and which only found its true worldwide audience on the secondary medium of home-video. So when I was asked to write and present a Channel Four documentary to accompany a screening of *The Shawshank Redemption*, it was toward the audience reaction that I turned my attention, convinced that there must be *some* reason why such an apparently innocuous film was having such a profound effect on so many disparate viewers. It was during the course of making that documentary, produced and directed by Russell Leven and Andrew Abbott respectively, that I first encountered the quasi-religious interpretation of Frank Darabont's movie which I have explored in this volume, and which may go *some* way toward explaining its extraordinary appeal.

The Shawshank Redemption began life as a novella, one of four 'ordinary stories' by horror guru Stephen King, published in the 1982 anthology *Different Seasons* which also included *The Body*, filmed by Rob Reiner as *Stand By Me*. Originally entitled *Rita Hayworth and Shawshank Redemption*, this was a departure from scary fare like *Carrie* and *The Shining* which had made King a household name. Written in the aftermath of *The Dead Zone*, and described by its author as 'a prison-break story in the grainy old Warner Brothers/Jimmy Cagney mold',[1] *Rita Hayworth and Shawshank Redemption* was a fairy tale of incarceration and emancipation in which an abused prisoner triumphs over terrible adversity by escaping into dreams of the movies – both literally and metaphorically.

Characterising himself as in, rather than *of*, the movie business ever since Brian De Palma's *Carrie* had become a box-office hit in the 1970s, King had developed an unusually charitable policy of optioning his shorter stories to budding film students for a mere one dollar, on the condition that they weren't screened commercially and he retained the rights. 'Talent or lack of it rarely made any difference to me,' explained King. 'I was trying to pay back a little of what I had been given over the years – hours of happiness in the dark.'[2] Although many of the resultant student experiments were, by King's own admission, unworthy of more than a single viewing, Frank Darabont's adaptation of *The Woman in the Room*, from the anthology *Night Shift*, impressed the author greatly – a film which left King 'in slack-jawed amazement' at its treatment of a story which 'had been written as a kind of cry from the heart after my mother's long losing battle with cervical cancer had finally ended'.[3] Thus his interest was piqued when, many years later, Darabont approached him again regarding the feature option rights for *Rita Hayworth and Shawshank Redemption.*

For Darabont, who had by now racked up screen credits on such second-rate horror fare as the 1980s' remake of *The Blob* and the *sequel* to the remake of *The Fly* (and who, according to close friend David Schow, was now apparently facing the possibility of making his directorial feature debut with a 'Chucky-type' shocker[4]), *Rita Hayworth and Shawshank Redemption* offered the possibility of moving more toward the work of Frank Capra, whose films he loved. As Darabont explains in *Shawshank: The Redeeming Feature*:

I grew up with Norman Rockwell and Frank Capra, and there's a part of me that's completely captivated by those kinds of storytellers who would tell those kinds of 'tall tales'. Some of the best 'tall tales' I've ever heard came from Capra – *Mr Smith Goes to Washington*, for example, is nothing if not a tall tale. *It's a Wonderful Life* is even taller. So I've always described *The Shawshank Redemption* not as a prison movie but as a 'tall tale'.

In his introduction to Darabont's published screenplay for *The Shawshank Redemption*, King remembers that he first thought it read like the kind of work that no film-maker could reasonably expect to get made: low on action; heavy on characterisation; and featuring 'Hoary old devices that should not work – Morgan Freeman's ubiquitous voice-overs, for instance'.[5] Yet by the time pre-production began in January 1993, the general consensus (shared by King) was that this was an unusually accomplished script, a 'hot property' which was now attracting the attention of A-list stars such as Nic Cage and Tom Cruise. Encouraging too was the support of Castle Rock, whose existence had been founded on the unlikely success of *Stand By Me*, and who King

A heritage of horror: Darabont and King

later credited with rescuing 'my film-associated reputation from the scrap-heap'.[6]

Released in theatres in 1994, *Shawshank* initially garnered little public attention, despite some glowing reviews and widespread high-brow acclaim. Indeed in its initial release period, the movie recouped only $18 million of its $35 million investment; this at a time when blockbusters were regularly taking upward of $100 million. Not even seven Oscar nominations could help it compete with the success of films like *Speed*, *Pulp Fiction* or *Forrest Gump*, which were then setting the standard for hit box-office status, and in whose shadow *Shawshank* seemed utterly dwarfed. As Morgan Freeman would later admit:

I don't know *what* happened to it when it came out. I remember someone asking me on the night of the Academy Awards why I thought *The Shawshank Redemption* had done very poorly at the box office, while *Dumb & Dumber*, which opened the same season, had done very well. Because whereas *Shawshank* had got pretty good reviews, *Dumb & Dumber* had been thoroughly and relentlessly trashed by critics.[7]

Frank Darabont lines up a shot

More unexpected than its box-office failure, however, was the unprecedented resurrection which *The Shawshank Redemption* would subsequently enjoy on video, where it bucked all marketing trends and predictions to become one of the top-renting tapes of 1995. According to Brian Jamieson of Warner Home Video, the film actually shipped 320,000 units on rental video in the US, an unusually strong showing which was 'kinda out of whack' with its poor box-office results. And it was on video that *Shawshank* began to win its most ardent fans, watched and loved in the privacy of the home (rather than the public arena of the movie theatre) and then recommended through word of mouth to a growing army of fans. Founder and Managing Director of the Internet Movie Database Col Needham reports that nearly one million voters have contributed to their poll which now places the film alongside *The Godfather* and *Star Wars* as the best of all time, and suggests that a majority of those who voted for *Shawshank* almost certainly saw it on video. Even more unusual is the profound impact which the film seems to have had on some viewers, particularly those who see it as a modern allegory for personal and spiritual salvation. As David Bruce, from the exotically named website HollywoodJesus.com, observes: 'It's an example of film as therapy. *Shawshank Redemption* gives you hope: you *can* go on; you *can* go forward.' But although the film may seem on one level to suggest a primarily religious 'redemption', it is also, as we shall see, an exemplary escape fantasy which allows for a whole range of 'exits' from the horrors of confinement or repression; playing with models of revolutionary transformation, making an almost Nietzschean leap 'beyond good and evil', and celebrating the consummate escape machine of cinema itself. Outlandish claims perhaps, but claims which seem peculiarly borne out by the hundreds of personal testimonies now posted on the Internet, proclaiming the weirdly healing properties of *The Shawshank Redemption*. Prison drama, political tract, modern gospel or cinematic fantasy? Salvation, as Warden Norton says, lies within.

1 Deus ex Machina: The Sacred Projector

The Shawshank Redemption opens to the sounds of the Ink Spots singing the popular and instantly recognisable romantic ballad 'If I Didn't Care' over the Castle Rock logo. As the credits begin, we see a bedraggled Andy Dufresne (Tim Robbins) sitting in a '46 Plymouth outside the house in which his wife is committing adultery. As the valve radio warbles away, filling the air with the sound of close-harmony crooning, Andy's hand reaches into the glove compartment for a gun and bullets wrapped in an oily rag, a bottle of Rosewood liquor cradled in his lap. From here, we cut to the bright interior of a courtroom where the District Attorney confronts the now shockingly sober Dufresne with the accusation that he told his recently murdered wife '"I'll see you in Hell before I see you Reno." Those were the words you used, Mr Dufresne, according to the testimony of your neighbours'. 'If they say so,' replies Dufresne in a state of almost catatonic serenity. 'I really don't remember. I was upset.'

Following his claim that he went to the house of his wife's golf-pro lover 'mostly to scare them', we cut back to the night of the crime to see the 'confused, drunk' Andy loading bullets into his revolver (actually Darabont doing his own hand-doubling pick-ups), a look of anguished resolution on his face. According to Andy he then returned home, throwing his gun into the Royal River, a turn of events which the prosecutor describes as 'convenient' since it cannot be matched with the weapon which killed the lovers, but which Andy stoically deems 'decidedly inconvenient ... since I am innocent of this crime'. A few moments later, as Andy's spatted feet are seen in close-up stumbling from the car, broken glass and bullets crushed underfoot, we hear the DA summing up his case, conceding to the jury that the lovers 'had sinned', but asking them to consider whether 'their crime [was] so great as to merit a death sentence?' As Andy is convicted, and condemned to serve 'two life sentences ... one for each of your victims', the judge's gavel comes down and the screen fades to black.

Although Darabont's original screenplay depicted Andy Dufresne's 'crime' as a pre-credits sequence, with the subsequent trial then playing out through the opening titles, judicious post-production editing conflated these two sequences into a more punchy opening which economically sets up many of the recurrent themes which will haunt *The Shawshank Redemption*. Most significantly, Andy's alleged declaration that he will see his wife 'in hell', and the DA's casual acceptance that the deceased 'had sinned' establishes from the very outset the quasi-theological environment in which the unfolding drama will play out. Even the most casual viewer of *The Shawshank Redemption* may be struck by the repetitively religious tone of the dialogue, in which biblical judgments are invoked at every turn, and each profanity tends more toward blasphemy than sexual vulgarity. In his first words in the film, Red swears by 'God's honest truth'; Captain Hadley invokes 'God and Sonny Jesus' when threatening to send every man to the infirmary on Andy's first night in Shawshank; Heywood exclaims 'Sweet Jesus!' when he learns of Andy's innocence; Haig declares '*Oh my Holy God!*' on discovering Dufresne's miraculous disappearance; even the demonic Warden Norton, who professes to have 'no blasphemy' in his prison, sarcastically screams 'Lord it's a miracle!' when faced with his own undoing. Although such religious epithets may be in keeping with the film's period setting (at least in its early stages), their constant repetition has a cumulative effect upon the viewer, suggesting one possible interpretation of the drama.

Another key signifier introduced at this early stage is memory, or more significantly the *lack* of it. Apparently an irrelevant throwaway comment designed (perhaps) to cover a guilty truth, Andy's aside 'I really don't remember' in fact raises an issue which will become profoundly significant for the prisoner – the transience of memory as an allegory for forgiveness. Years later, revealing his dream of escaping to Zihuatanejo, the incarcerated Andy will tell Red of his longing for 'a warm place that has no memory', a vision of paradise manifested in the form of a coastal resort flanking the Pacific Ocean.

Most significant, however, is the clear implication from this opening sequence that Andy Dufresne is guilty. Although cine-literate viewers may be inclined from the outset to believe that the absence of a clear-cut murder scene signals a gap in our knowledge of events, the circumstantial evidence

Drunk, armed and convicted: Andy gets life

definitely fingers Dufresne as the killer of his wife and her lover. In stark contrast to King's source, in which Red announces from the outset that Andy Dufresne was one of fewer than ten Shawshank inmates he considered to be innocent, Darabont's movie allows Red to describe Andy as a convicted murderer whose guilt we are encouraged to accept. This is important for two reasons. First, from the outset we are asked to accept Andy as a form of 'justified sinner', a man who has been driven to murderous acts by the iniquities of his situation perhaps, but still a murderer nonetheless. (Later on, Andy will tell Red that 'on the outside I was an honest man … I had to come to prison to be a crook'.) Second, in an environment in which 'everyone in here is innocent' (the recurrent chant of the Shawshank inmates), Andy's assumed 'guilt' puts him on a par with the men in whose company he will be forced to spend the next twenty-odd years. In particular, it creates a bond between Andy and Red, who describes himself as 'the only guilty man in Shawshank', and whose acceptance of his own guilt will later prove to be his very salvation. In a drama in which so much is made of the nature of innocence, there is a marked difference between portraying Dufresne as simply a wronged man and depicting him as fallen soul, sympathetic but still guilty. In Darabont's film, it is essential that we do not dismiss Andy as the former but accept him as the latter; a good man tainted with the stench of death who has yet to achieve redemption.

Up for Rejection

Having established Andy Dufresne as the central figure in his unfolding drama, Darabont now takes us through the bars of Shawshank prison, where he conducts an abrupt volte-face and introduces us to the true 'hero' of the story. Seen attending a parole-board hearing after serving twenty years of a life sentence, Red (Morgan Freeman) is presented at first as a naive innocent, protesting his salvation with a blinking eagerness that hints at duplicity ('I can honestly say that I'm a changed man'). As the camera closes in for a 'REJECTED' stamp on his parole document (which incidentally bears a photograph of Freeman's son Alfonso, and names the prisoner as 'Ellis Boyd Redding'), we cut to Red re-entering Shawshank's prison yard, now carrying himself with the demeanour of a world-weary

Wide-eyed, rejected and resigned: Red fails parole

con, simply going through the 'same old shit, diff'rent day'. In this environment, everyone is 'up for rejection next week', a patina of gallows-humour glossing the purgatorial nature of their situation in which salvation is little more than a hollow joke.

With Red now revealed as a player, surrounded by prisoners eager for his services, we hear for the first time the captivating voice-over which will define this as *his* story (despite his protestations in the novella that 'it's not me I want to tell you about'[8]). Slightly paraphrasing the opening lines from *Rita Hayworth and Shawshank Redemption*, Freeman's deliciously luxurious voice addresses the audience directly with the words, 'There must be a con like me in every prison in America. I'm the guy who can get it for you.' As he speaks, cinematographer Roger Deakins sneaks a long shot across the exercise yard, overcranking slightly to create an almost subliminal sense of slow motion as Red and his squat companion stroll through the crowd, a sleight of hand allowing the passing of contraband between them as they swagger like a sheriff and his deputy in a B-movie Western. Just then, a siren announcing the arrival of 'fresh fish' breaks into the couple's silent reverie as we segue into what Darabont describes as 'everybody's favourite shot in the movie',[9] an astonishing aerial view of Shawshank prison which gives us, for the first time, a sense of the awesome landscape in which this drama will be played out.

'Welcome to Shawshank'

Although *Rita Hayworth* is set, like so much of King's fiction, in the relatively idyllic surroundings of Maine, New England, Darabont's movie was shot in Mansfield, Ohio, the proud possessor of an extraordinary building which would become a defining character in *The Shawshank Redemption.* Originally the site of Camp Mordecai Bailey, a Union training base for civil war soldiers, this looming landmark – which is known interchangeably as Mansfield Reformatory and The Ohio State Reformatory – is one part cathedral, two parts Castle Frankenstein. Designed by architect Levi T. Scofield, a native of Cleveland who had travelled widely in Europe, the building is correctly described by tour guide and guardian angel Jan Demyan as 'an odd mixture of architectural

'Everybody's favourite shot': welcome to Shawshank

styles; it's Richardsonian Romanesque, chateau-esque, and also gothic in the overtones of the interior'.[10] According to Demyan, the architecture is specifically designed to draw the eyes skywards, suggesting to those who walk its halls and corridors that they are in a church.

From the state authorities' point of view, these peculiarly religious overtones exactly fitted their designs for the building, which, from 1896 to 1990, functioned as a reformatory which attempted to combine the fortressed needs of a prison with the evangelising zeal of a correctional facility. Mansfield is a religious town, a place where today the greatest tourist attraction (other than the Reformatory) is a waxwork museum depicting scenes from the Bible, and where meals are served in restaurants in which every attention is given to family seating, and very little to the availability of alcohol. (Tim Robbins remembers Mansfield as 'a very dull Midwestern town, very religious', and jokes that they ended up staying in the house of 'a Seventh Day Adventist dentist'.) This combination of architectural elements would also make Mansfield Reformatory the perfect setting for a tale of spiritual redemption spun by two masters of the macabre (King and Darabont), both of whom had learned their trade in the horror genre. As Warden Norton says, 'I believe in two things,

Darabont directs Andy's arrival at Shawshank

discipline and the Bible. Here you will receive both. Put your trust in the Lord, your ass belongs to me. Welcome to Shawshank.'

Picking up the white prison bus as it turns left onto the approach road toward Shawshank, 'everybody's favourite shot' climbs from a low angle to a dizzying height as it scales the castle's gothic turrets, banking slightly to the left as it clears the observation tower, picking out the hundred-odd extras in the yard before circling and escaping over the side wall, a Maine State flag snapping briskly in the icy breeze. According to Darabont, the trajectory of this shot, which 'seems to suspend time even as it plunges us breathlessly into this new and horrible world',[11] came from production designer Terence Marsh, who muttered during an early scouting trip to Mansfield that 'This place would look smashing with an opening helicopter shot.'[12] Operated by cameraman Mike Kelem, this aerial view is also notable for creating the impression that the Ohio State Reformatory was in a functioning state of repair at the time of the *Shawshank* shoot, a deft act of cinematic deception considering that the building was in line for demolition, and indeed reportedly would have kept an appointment with a wrecking ball had not Hollywood stardom bestowed iconic status upon it.

Fresh Fish and First Night

Having established the specific date of 1947 for Andy's induction into Shawshank (*Rita Hayworth* plumps for 1948), Darabont offers us views of the prison inmates pressing up against barbed-wired fences, the uniformed guards swathed with mildly fetishistic leather accoutrements, sneering and battering as the 'Human Charm Bracelet'[13] files defeatedly off the coach and into the delousing arena. Immediately the taunts begin, with the hardened cons taking horse-bets on who will crack first: the 'little sack of shit' up front, or the 'chubby fat ass' dragging his weight in terror. Red, always with an eye for an edge, puts his money on the 'tall drink of water with a silver spoon up his ass', the first oblique reference to the rape and sexual torment which Andy (and his fellow fresh fish) will suffer in Shawshank.

The rapidity and forthrightness with which the theme of sexual abuse is established and explored is particularly unusual for a film which

Showered, powdered and stripped: 'women-in-prison' style exploitation of Andy

has developed such a reputation for mainstream palatability. Indeed, on first viewing, one could be forgiven for imagining that *The Shawshank Redemption* was actually far too tough and uncompromising in its depiction of male rape to court widespread acceptance. From the moment he steps through the Reformatory's imposing entrance arch and into Shawshank's reception hall (where one can still find traces of the set dresser's yellow-painted line) it seems that the primary threat to Andy is sexual rather than judicial. Even his encounter with the maniacal Warden Norton, who declares that 'your ass belongs to me', bears forebodingly penetrative overtones, tensions which are heightened in the subsequent shots of a naked and caged Dufresne being violently hosed, deloused and frog-marched unclothed through the cell-block corridors. (If this were a women-in-prison movie, the tone of exploitation would be both familiar and titillatory). Like dead men awakening in purgatory, the naked inmates discover their 'old life blown away in the blink of an eye, nothing left but all the time in the world to think about it …'

Before we examine further the horrors of that first night, it is worth noting that the interior cell blocks, which are now intercut with haunting night-time exteriors of Shawshank, are in fact a vast set, constructed to Terence Marsh's specifications in a studio a few miles from Mansfield Reformatory. In reality, the rabbit warrens of prison cells at Mansfield face outward from a central stack (rather than inward as in the film), and were in such a state of disrepair by 1993 as to make filming virtually impossible. It is on Marsh's set, therefore, that we see the lights go down on Andy's first night, and begin to hear the jeering 'fresh fish' cries of the inmates which will drive 'Fat Ass' to dementia and (by extension) to death. 'I know a couple of big ol' bull queers who'd just *love* to make your acquaintance,' leers Heywood, ironically one of the more likeable characters in Shawshank, 'especially that big white mushy butt of yours …' When his quarry cracks, screaming 'God I don't belong here!', we are reminded again of the parallels between Shawshank and purgatory, a place where the prayers of the damned go unheeded. As Hadley pulls Fat Ass from his cell and beats him to a pulp with his night-stick (ironically invoking, as we noted previously, 'God and Sonny Jesus'), the cells fall silent, and Red is

Shooting in Terence Marsh's vast cell-block set

seen through prison bars retreating wordlessly into the darkness. Andy, we learn, never made a sound – in fact, he seems to remain silent until the next day when he becomes a sole voice asking if anyone knew (the now deceased) Fat Ass's name. No one does.

Sex and The Sisters

The sexual torments continue after breakfast as Andy Dufresne is singled out by Bogs, the most villainous of 'The Sisters' – Shawshank's resident rapists – whom Red later warns have taken a liking to Andy. In a section in Stephen King's short story which begins 'A few words about the sisters', King outlines in detail the homosexual coupling in Shawshank which 'like straight sex, comes in a hundred different shapes and forms'.[14] Describing in an admirably even tone the pseudo 'gay' relationships which flourish behind bars, King's narrator observes that 'there's a lot of buggery going on inside the walls': from the men who 'come out of the closet'[15] and discover their true sexuality during incarceration; to a physical 'arrangement between two fundamentally heterosexual men'[16] who simply *need* sex in one form or another. As for The Sisters, however, King's Red is at pains to point out that 'They are to prison society what the rapist is to the society outside the walls', stressing that for them 'the joy has always been in taking it by force'.[17]

This discussion is compacted and clarified somewhat by Darabont's adaptation, in which Andy asks if he would be safe from The Sisters 'if I explained to them that I'm not homosexual?', to which Red replies blankly: 'Neither are they. You have to be human first. They don't qualify. Bull queers take by force. It's all they want or understand.' A short time later, Andy is seen failing to fight off an attack by The Sisters, who corner him in the laundry stockroom and (presumably) proceed to gang-rape him. Although handled with a degree of visual tact, this sequence is explicit enough to leave the viewer in little doubt as to the nature of the attack, a brutal truth driven home by Freeman's voice-over, which intones, 'I wish I could tell you that Andy fought the good fight and The Sisters let him be … but prison is no fairy-tale world.'

The rapes continue through a montage sequence in which scenes of a bruised and battered Andy silently walking the snowy exercise yard are intercut with yet more footage of The Sisters setting upon their prey. 'Sometimes he was able to fight them off,' says Red. 'Sometimes not ...' What is unusual (perhaps even extraordinary) about these sequences is the deft, almost casual manner in which Darabont manages to make the spectre of male rape if not normal, then at least unremarkable. Remember that, during the early 1970s, films such as John Boorman's *Deliverance* and John Schlesinger's *Midnight Cowboy* were considered almost outrageously liberal for depicting anal rape between men in anything but the most oblique terms. Even in the late 1980s, big-screen prison dramas such as Peter Yates' execrable *An Innocent Man* were proving that not even Tom Selleck could sell a film which featured or dealt with the issue of male rape. How remarkable, then, that *The Shawshank Redemption*, which is not widely remembered for its frank sexual forthrightness, should handle such potentially controversial material in such a remarkably matter-of-fact manner. Some of the credit for this is due to Stephen King, in whose novella Red talks freely about his *own* experiences of buggery in Shawshank, commenting casually that 'The bleeding really is like a menstrual flow; it keeps up for two, maybe three days, a slow trickle. Then it stops. No harm done'. The comparison with menstruation is intriguing because, while reducing the physical harm of anal rape to the level of a normalised form of blood loss, it also clearly feminises the narrator, casting him momentarily as a woman stoically dealing with one of the more unpalatable facts of life. A similar feminisation of Andy Dufresne occurs during *The Shawshank Redemption*, leaving him to confront an issue which has haunted women-in-prison movies since the drive-in days of Roger Corman. For, as Red concludes, 'rape is rape, and eventually you have to look at your face in the mirror again and decide what to make of yourself.'[18]

It is worth noting, too, that Darabont clearly went out of his way to transpose the complex sexual miasma of King's short story to the screen without making the usual compromises inherent in the transition to 'mainstream' entertainment. Although it would clearly have been easier either to have written The Sisters out of his script, or simply to allow Andy Dufresne to escape their advances, Darabont makes a point of depicting

Andy as a rape victim – not once, but on several occasions – and addressing the relationship (or lack of it) between consensual and *non*-consensual sodomy. In his notes to the published screenplay of *The Shawshank Redemption*, Darabont states clearly that 'Both the novella and the film take pains to draw a distinction between a homosexual and a prison rapist', going on to explain that 'the prison rapist is seldom a homosexual in the outside world – what he is, is a damn *rapist*.' As if this were not clear enough, the writer/director feels obliged to state 'one last time for the record: Bogs as a character does not represent homosexuality; he represents the predatory sexual violence of rape.'[19]

When Andy Met Red

Although some uncharitable souls have read Darabont's forceful defence of his depiction of Bogs and The Sisters as an after-the-fact attempt to escape charges of homophobia, a less simplistic reading of *The Shawshank Redemption* clearly characterises it as unusually sympathetic to the many levels of sexual tension and partnership which exist in male relationships. Indeed, one clear reason for preserving the character of Bogs the rapist in all his predatory horror is to highlight a growing, positive facet of the relationship between Andy and Red, which, although devoid of sexual contact, looks more like a blossoming love affair with each frame of film. In *Shawshank: The Redeeming Feature*, Morgan Freeman explicitly defines the story as 'a sort of love relationship between Red and Andy' which 'did go deeper than just friendship'. Similarly, in his *Viewfinder* interview for FilmFour, Tim Robbins surmised that one of the two main reasons why *The Shawshank Redemption* has such a profound effect upon so many viewers is the fact that 'it's a film in which you actually see a relationship between two men which isn't based on car chases, or scoring some women, or some kind of "caper".' Although stressing in passing that Red and Andy's relationship was clearly chaste, Robbins went on to conclude that 'the *possibility* of that non-sexual friendship happening between two men is, I think, one of the reasons why that film is so revered. Because I don't think we're given that model in many other films.'[20]

This model friendship begins in the film (as in the novella) during an encounter in the recreation yard when Andy sidles up to Red and asks him to procure a rock hammer with which he can begin to carve and chisel the quartz, mica and shale littered around the courtyard floor. Opening with a few overtly flirty glances before Andy plucks up the courage to approach Red, who is busily throwing ball with his buddies, this brightly lit meeting has a levity of tone and a hint of arousal which is only a heartbeat away from a high-school movie encounter between an enigmatic new-girl-at-school and a rugged, popular jock. Referring to Andy (to his face) as the 'wife killin' banker' (his possible 'innocence' being laughed off as nothing more than a joke), Red subtly puffs up his own importance while teasingly extricating personal details about Andy's 'old life'. All this, while still stoically playing catch with his buddies, feigning disinterest but clearly tickled pink to have been picked out from the crowd. (Darabont reports that Morgan Freeman's throwing arm nearly fell off during the day's shooting it took to get this scene in the can.[21]) Most telling of all is Red's lingering look as the scene reaches its humorous punch-line, a distant stare which breaks into a barely suppressed grin as Andy walks (or more accurately shimmies) away, the pair's eyes meeting once again at a distance as Andy teasingly turns back to ensure that he *is* being watched. And over this, like a kid with a crush, we hear Red admitting, 'Yeah, I think it would be fair to say I liked Andy from the start …'

A note here on the casting of Morgan Freeman, and the 'big joke' which results from his landing the key role of 'Red'. In Stephen King's novella, the narrator is clearly intended to be a white man of Irish descent, and it was with such a character in mind that Darabont wrote his screenplay adaptation. According to the director, when the African-American actor Morgan Freeman's name was initially mooted for Red, he was first startled, then immediately converted. Rather than rewriting the script to accommodate the colour-change of the character, Darabont simply inserted a gag about the origin of Red's nickname which has become the funniest line in the film.

In *Rita Hayworth and Shawshank Redemption*, when Andy asks how Red happens to come by 'certain items', the old lag sardonically replies that 'things just seem to come into my hand. I can't explain it. Unless it's because I'm Irish.'[22] Although this exchange is paraphrased in Darabont's published screenplay (written before the casting of Morgan Freeman), the finished film contains instead a wry aside in which Andy asks, 'Red – why do they call you that?', provoking a marvellously mischievous pause from Freeman, who gazes quizzically into the middle distance before answering, 'Maybe it's because I'm Irish …' What is notable about this gag, which comes at the end of one of the most emotionally significant scenes in the film, is that it marks the only instance in which Red the character (as opposed to Red the narrator) breaks the fourth wall and effectively winks at the audience. Although the omnipresence of his voice-over places Red in a privileged position, allowing him to talk directly to the viewer, the laws of convention prevent his on-screen presence from ever acknowledging the audience. Yet here, fleetingly, are Freeman, Robbins, and of course Darabont, giving us a discreetly knowing nudge, momentarily breaking the 'reality' of the drama, reminding us of their role as storytellers, as creators of the unfolding drama.

As for Robbins, his casting seems to have been inspired partly by the strong sense of vulnerability which he displayed in Adrian Lyne's underrated fantasy thriller *Jacob's Ladder*, which exhibits more parallels with *The Shawshank Redemption* than may at first be apparent. Like Darabont's feature debut, *Jacob's Ladder* performed disappointingly in cinemas, only coming to the attention of viewers on video, where it became a highly regarded and rentable cult title. More important, however, is the somewhat unearthly quality which Robbins brings to the role of Jacob Singer, who is revealed ultimately as a man in the throes of death, trapped somewhere between this world and the next. This sense of being a man at one remove from the material world is central to the character of Andy Dufresne, whom Darabont compares to a 'Joseph Campbell mythic hero, the stranger who rides out of the desert, cleans up the town, then rides away'.[23]

Clearly there are comparisons between Dufresne and the 'pale rider' of Western lore, an iconic figure frequently characterised as ghostly, the whiff of the undead following in his wake. Of Andy, Red comments that 'He strolled like a man in a park without a care or a worry in the world,

like he had on an invisible coat that would shield him from this place.' The nature of this 'invisible coat' is clearly open to numerous interpretations, ranging from Andy's oft-noted 'cold fish' qualities to the more extraordinary possibility of spiritual protection, a halo-like quality which engulfs and enfolds him. For those who care to see Andy as a Christ-like figure, this observation is particularly important, for it suggests that Dufresne is only partly of this earth, a displaced angel traipsing through the dirt of the world, untarnished by its imperfection. Add to this Red's declaration in King's novella that his first meeting with Dufresne took place 'on a Sunday',[24] and the opportunities to interpret Andy as a latter-day Jesus are yet further multiplied.

The look of love

The Lords of All Creation

In the spring of 1949, after almost two years of harassment by The Sisters, Red manages discreetly to save Andy's life, a favour which his friend will later return in spades. According to Red's voice-over, the routine of rape and humiliation which Andy had endured was becoming unbearable, to the extent that 'if things had gone on that way, this place would've got the best of him'. Rather than offering a comforting ear or ministering advice, Red uses what he is best at – an understanding of the black market – to fix it for himself and a few of his friends to be among the twelve inmates assigned to tar the licence-plate factory roof; outdoor work which comes as a blessing in the 'damn fine' month of May. The price that each chosen inmate pays is a pack of cigarettes, with Red taking his usual 20 per cent commission – a significant rewriting of the scenario in King's novella, in which Andy and Red simply 'happened' to be assigned together. While this elaboration may at first seem incidental, the fact that what happens up on that roof, in both the book and the film, proves to be Andy's salvation lends a significance to the manner of its contrivance. Specifically, in Darabont's film, Red is *responsible* (albeit inadvertently) for putting Andy in the path of his own redemption, and therefore becomes his unwitting saviour.

It is up on the roof, in the noonday sun, that Andy overhears the wretched Captain Hadley bitching about the inheritance tax he is about to

Andy in Christ-like pose on the licence-plate factory roof

pay on money left to him by his rich brother, and asks him enigmatically if he trusts his wife. From a vertiginous overhead shot which swoops down from the heavens to meet Hadley holding Dufresne in a deliberately Christ-like pose, we see Andy calmly cutting a life-saving deal even as he teeters on the edge of a precipitous drop. To the astonishment of guards and inmates alike, Andy tells Hadley that he can gift his inheritance tax-free to his wife, an operation which would require his services to do the paperwork, and would cost only 'three beers apiece for each of my co-workers – I think a man working outdoors feels more like a man if he can have a bottle of suds'. Cut from here, via some brief transitional shots, to the sight of the sun-beaten cons, silently sucking on 'icy-cold Bohemia-style beer' (both novella and script specify 'Black Label'), a wordless communion passing between them as they experience once again the almost alien feeling of being human. 'We sat and drank with the sun on our shoulders,' remembers Red as Thomas Newman's longingly discordant score swells, 'and felt like free men. Hell, we could've been tarring the roof of one of our own houses.' And then, in a crucial addition to dialogue lifted almost directly from the novella, Darabont inserts a final flourish, a parting prayer: 'We were the Lords of all creation.'

Although Darabont has subsequently informed me that no such parallels were intended, it is possible (should one so wish) to find powerful echoes of the Last Supper in this scene. Significantly, while King's novella calls for only 'nine or ten' men to be selected for roofing detail, and Darabont's script cites 'a dozen', a head-count of the inmates depicted in this sequence clearly reveals *thirteen* prisoners up on the roof, exactly mirroring the gathering of Jesus and the twelve disciples described in the Gospels. More strikingly still, both King's source and Darabont's adaptation make it clear that, having provided the blessed beer, 'Only Andy didn't drink',[25] a detail which fits neatly with the biblical descriptions of Jesus blessing, giving, but crucially not *partaking* of the wine which represents the first communion. Although there is some ambiguity in the English translations of Matthew and Mark, in which Jesus states either that he will not drink wine 'henceforth' (Matthew 26:29), or that he will 'drink no more' (Mark 14:25) until he is in the kingdom of heaven, there

is an unavoidable clarity of coincidence with Andy's provision of, and abstinence from, his gift of 'Bohemia-style beer' and Luke's description of Jesus handing the wine cup to his disciples with instructions to 'Take this and divide it among yourselves; For I say unto you I will not drink of the fruit of the vine until the kingdom of God shall come.' (22:17–18). Similarly, asked if he 'want[s] a cold one?' Andy merely smiles benignly and replies 'No thanks, I gave up drinking ...'

King's narrator also takes this moment openly to discuss the birth of Andy as a legend rather than as a mere man, joking that hundreds of men must have been up on that roof judging by the number claiming to have witnessed this miraculous event, and concluding that Dufresne possessed

Second sitting for the Last Supper: Andy watches as the disciples drink

'a kind of inner light he carried around with him'[26] which would inspire stories of his escapades long after his departure. Here, the biblical parallels seem both clear and intentional, drawing our attention subtly toward the creation of the messianic myth which flourished *after* Jesus' lifetime, and through which the disciples and their descendants became both the keepers and perhaps even the creators of the Christian flame. Just as Jesus was a man who literally lived through the Gospels, so Andy Dufresne, who is notably absent from King's story after his escape from Shawshank, lives in the stories of Red and his fellow inmates. 'To us long-timers who knew Andy over a space of years,' says King's narrator, 'there was an element of fantasy to him, a sense, almost, of myth magic, if you get what I mean.'[27] That Darabont gets what King 'means' seems unquestionable, as he beautifully conjures a second sitting for the Last Supper with Robbins 'hunkered in the shade, a strange little smile on his face', his beatific expression that of a man in quiet rapture, his exploits being recounted to us as a memory by the now disciple-like Red.

The Church of the Cinema

It is at about this point in *The Shawshank Redemption*, in the wake of Andy's rooftop communion, that the obliquely spiritual symbols begin to take on a more explicit form. But rather than conforming to the straightforward latter-day gospel parallels which some have chosen to read into *Shawshank*'s overtly religious imagery, the film in fact emerges as a far more self-reflexive text, as it turns toward cinema itself as a prime space of both the spiritual and the sacred. From here on in, the secular nods which Darabont seems to make toward Christian myth are matched by a reverence for film and its icons which soon become talismanically central to the escape narrative underwriting *The Shawshank Redemption*. One can, for example, read the sight of Red admitting his own guilt while playing checkers with Andy (who now only mockingly professes innocence) as a nod to Ingmar Bergman's *The Seventh Seal*, with Morgan Freeman becoming a lowlier version of Max von Sydow's chess-playing knight, examining himself as he comes face to face with death. A moment later, as Andy finally begins to scratch his name on the wall of his cell, we see only the engraving of the letter A, suggesting *perhaps* the New Testament quotation 'I am Alpha and Omega', or maybe simply the first step, the first letter. (The carving of this letter is indeed later revealed to be the first glimmering of Andy's salvation, as he scratches his name on the wall, and the wall in turn begins to crumble.) Neither of these nods, however, bears the mark of deliberation, and both *may* indeed be either happy accidents or sheer coincidences, artistic quirks of which the writer/director is neither aware nor has an opinion.

But it is in the sequence in which Rita Hayworth finally makes an entrance in *The Shawshank Redemption* that the true religion of Darabont's movie becomes clear: a peculiar mix of Christian myth and cine-literate magic. As the inmates watch (with uncharacteristic solemnity) a projection of *Gilda* in a room which seems to double as a chapel, an excitedly anxious Andy leans over to ask Red if he can get Ms Hayworth for him. Although it is almost impossible to make out in the final cut, the projector's beam is in fact shining through a hole in a wall bedecked by a giant picture of the risen Jesus, the film literally beaming itself out of the body of Christ. (This painting is still very much in evidence in the ramshackle storeroom at Mansfield Reformatory where the sequence was shot.) Meanwhile, on the screen-within-the-screen, where *Gilda* is working its strangely perverse charms, we see the part 'where she does that shit with her hair' intercut with the unusually vibrant faces of the inmates, positively glowing with life-affirming *joie de vivre* as the projector beams its shaft of heavenly light

Ecstatic joy in the light of the projector

above their heads. 'God,' breathes Red in awe, 'I *love it* ...', an exclamation pitched somewhere between a prayer and an orgasm, before replying to Andy that in an environment like this he can indeed perform miracles, a response which seems entirely appropriate.

This sequence is crucial (perhaps even central) to the strange allure of *The Shawshank Redemption*, because it combines a nostalgia for the classic Hollywood film-making of which Darabont is so enamoured (*Gilda* was directed by Charles Vidor in the same year that Frank Capra was making *It's a Wonderful Life*) with an atmosphere of other-worldly transcendence. The 'message' of this sequence, later mirrored in the operatic broadcast which Andy mischievously relays throughout the prison, is that art can transform the nature of one's surroundings, taking us out of the here and now and transporting us to the Elysian fields of the imagination, making us again free men. Such freedom is literal in the case of Andy, who we later learn is looking for a poster of movie pin-up Rita Hayworth in order to cover his tracks as he tunnels his way out of his cell. For the moment, however, we are left to speculate on the suggestion inherent in King's novella surtitle 'Hope Springs Eternal' (later transformed into the movie's advertising tag-line 'Hope can set you free') that redemption is to be found in the church of the cinema, a place where dreams take flight, and where miracles become a reality rather than an abstraction.

In fact, in both King's novella and Darabont's original screenplay, the film that the inmates are watching is Billy Wilder's *The Lost Weekend*, another classic from the mid-1940s, in which Ray Milland discovers the evils of alcohol in hallucinatory fashion. According to Darabont, this title was due for inclusion in *The Shawshank Redemption* until a costing for clippage from Paramount Pictures turned out to be far too high for their modestly budgeted movie. Acting on the advice of producer Niki Marvin, Castle Rock instead approached Columbia Pictures, who held the domestic distribution rights for *The Shawshank Redemption*, and who promptly presented a list of lesser-priced titles, including a number featuring Rita Hayworth. Although in retrospect it seems obvious that a cine-literate film based on a novella entitled *Rita Hayworth and Shawshank Redemption* should feature *the* iconic scene from Hayworth's most

celebrated film, it was in fact only at this point that Darabont opted to go for *Gilda*, a decision which he would later refer to as a case of 'a smart producer turning a disadvantage into a strength and recognizing the creative potential'.[28]

Certainly, the peculiarly twisted sexuality of *Gilda* sits well with the tortured homoeroticism of *The Shawshank Redemption*: before Hayworth's dramatic entrance, we see Glenn Ford and George Macready discussing her in terms of a canary (caged like the prisoners), and note the ironic aside that it's 'quite a surprise to hear a woman singing in my house' (this in a prison full of men in which the company of women is notable only by its absence). The strangely sexual bond between Ford and Macready – homosocial if not homosexual – in which Hayworth becomes a commodified property, passed between the two male leads, also seems particularly significant in this context. But the fact that the film itself proved ultimately interchangeable with an alternative title (it could so easily have been *The Lost Weekend*) suggests that it is the *cinema*, rather than the specific *film*, which is the key element of this scene. In essence, what we see is a picture of men at worship, entranced by the magical light which dances above their heads, momentarily removed (by *whatever* film is playing) from the grim meat-hook realities of Shawshank prison. This is of crucial import to understanding Andy's ultimate escape, in which he will *literally* step through a movie poster to freedom, suggesting that the escapist possibilities of the medium are powerful enough to transcend physical reality. Perhaps *this* is the true 'religious' message playing at the heart of *The Shawshank Redemption*.

Later, in one of the few scenes which has no basis in King's novella, Darabont attempts to repeat and reinforce this theme of art (this time music) as a transforming beacon of hope with a sequence in which

Awe in the church of the cinema; and silenced by the magic of Mozart

Andy hijacks Warden Norton's public-address system and plays a record of a Mozart's *Marriage of Figaro* to the inmates. In *Shawshank: The Redeeming Feature*, Darabont states that the whole arc of the story 'can be seen in that one sequence in *Shawshank* when he plays the record for everyone in the prison and puts a completely new tone into things'. In his screenplay directions Darabont goes further, describing Andy's discovery of the disc of *Le nozze di Figaro* as 'the Grail … lilting and gorgeous' and stating that 'the numbing routine of prison life itself … all grinds to a stuttering halt [as] Everybody just stands in place, listening to the MUSIC, hypnotized'.[29]

On screen, things are every bit as hyperbolic as the screenplay suggests, the camera sweeping up in a majestic crane shot toward the exercise yard's loudspeaker, flying like a bird from the prison where the sick are inspired to climb out of their infirmary beds, as we hear the duet between Susanna and the Contessa which Darabont writes 'simply insisted on being in the movie'.[30] As Red says in reverent voice-over:

I have no idea to this day what those two Italian ladies were singing about … I like to think they were singing about something so beautiful it can't be expressed in words, and makes your heart ache because of it … It was like some beautiful bird flapped into our drab little cage and made those walls dissolve away. And for the briefest of moments every last man in Shawshank felt free.

(In fact, this is a case in which ignorance is bliss, because despite the beauty of the melody, the libretto is full of machinations and romantic intrigue, which Red cannot understand, and which are far from innocent.) Meanwhile, in Warden Norton's office, Andy beams the same beatific smile we saw playing on his face on the licence-factory roof, a reference which clearly links these two superhuman acts of giving, reconfirming Andy's role as the spiritual saviour of Shawshank's inmates.

Although this sequence has proved to be a favourite with fans of the movie, it is one of only two sequences in *The Shawshank Redemption* which I find uncomfortable or consider misjudged. The problem is partly one of the message being inseparable from the medium. (When Heywood later complains to Andy that 'You couldn't play something good, huh? Hank Williams?', my sympathies are entirely with him, as I believe would be those of the other inmates.) More troublesome, however, is the fact that this sequence seems somewhat inorganic, imposed upon (rather than growing from) the drama in order to make a specific point. While it is arguable that audiences have ultimately proved Darabont right (many viewers of *The Shawshank Redemption* refer to this sequence in uplifting terms), Andy's subsequent declaration that he managed to survive the two weeks in solitary because he had 'Mr Mozart to keep me company', while tapping his heart and head, seem to this author overly explanatory, particularly when it is followed by the announcement that 'there's something inside that they can't get to, can't touch … Hope.'

Compare the relative clumsiness of this celebrated sequence with the complex understatement of Red's moment of wonderment in the cinema, when the simple vision of Rita Hayworth shaking her hair provokes a far more believable and spontaneous outpouring of joy. How fitting, too, that this marvellously cinematic moment should precede a showdown with The Sisters in which Andy finally manages to reassert his dignity within the hallowed sanctuary of the projection booth. Cornered as he leaves the auditorium and bundled violently among the reels of film, Andy finds himself facing his worst enemies in a symbolic arena wherein the various themes of the film reach a dramatic intersection. It is here that a brief but extraordinary three-way conversation takes place between Andy, Bogs and the soundtrack of *Gilda*, a fleeting moment of movie magic in which the godlike voice of the film (*Gilda*) seems to speak directly to its audience (Hayworth devotee Andy) as he finally squares up to confront his demons (Bogs and co., all blind and deaf to the magic of cinema).

Although the central thrust of the following scene and some of the dialogue is taken directly from King's novella, the location and symbolic significance of Andy's profoundly cinematic victory over Bogs and his crew are Darabont's own, and represent some of the most rewarding invention of the entire film. 'What are you supposed to say to the bride?' burbles the now off-screen *Gilda* significantly as Bogs leers lovingly at

Andy, ready again to rape him. 'Ain't you gonna scream?' asks Bogs in a whisper. 'Good luck,' answers the movie, clear as a bell, a comment that could be directed at either protagonist, but which seems to spur Andy into decisive action. Turning away from Bogs in what looks initially like submission, Andy bends toward a stack of film reels as Hayworth is faintly overheard trilling, 'My husband tells me you're a great believer …' (Although the occurrence of these stray line *seems* random, it is worth remembering that they were almost certainly dubbed in post-production, and thus were probably chosen with some care and purpose.) Then, in the words of Darabont's screenplay, Dufresne 'curls his fingers around a full 1,000 foot reel of 35mm film'[31] which he then smashes violently into Bogs' and Rooster's faces, breaking the latter's nose in the process. It is the beginning of the end for Bogs, and also humorous proof of the power of celluloid to affect material change.

A scuffle and a beating ensue, during which Andy is forced (arms once again outstretched in cruciform mode) to his knees. In such a symbolically heightened atmosphere, the obscenity of Bogs' leering threats now takes on an edge of blasphemy as he pulls a knife from his pocket and intones, 'I'm gonna open my fly and you're gonna swallow what I give you to swallow.' Once again, the explicitness of Bogs' words (which come directly from King) strike home as genuinely alarming and outrageous, hardly the stuff of 'feel-good' fare, and certainly a million miles away from the sanitised sexuality of most allegedly comparable Hollywood fodder. Equally uncomfortable is the hint of perverse communion with which Darabont infests this scene, placing the increasingly demonic Bogs in the role of virtual Antichrist, administering sadistic black mass to his sacrificial victim.

'Anything you put in my mouth you're gonna lose.' With this phrase the entire dynamic of the scene begins to change, with Andy's impending victory suddenly registering as a triumph of spirit over matter. Looking Bogs in the eye and calmly explaining that sticking a knife in his ear will simply cause him to bite down hard through reflex action, Andy offers a repeat performance of his rooftop besting of Hadley when, according to King, 'Andy simply *forced* him' to submit to his strength of will.[32] In a

nicely fanciful flourish, apparently added *after* the locking of the shooting
script, Darabont also takes the opportunity to acknowledge the power of
literature alongside the mystery of cinema, allowing Andy to taunt Bogs
with the fact that he has *read* about the bite-reflex, and asking, 'You know
how to *read*, you ignorant fuck?'

The beating that follows is savage in both novella and film, with the
key difference being that, in the movie, Andy avoids being raped, a
clarification of his unilateral victory over The Sisters in what has become,
in Darabont's version, a thematically critical episode. Further significance
is piled upon the scene as Bogs spends a week in solitary (which looks for
all the world like a toilet cubicle) before returning to his cell, where he is

Andy triumphs over Bogs in the shadow of *Gilda*

promptly battered to within an inch of his life by Hadley and his longtime cohort Mert. Although the novella includes this assault, and its permanently disabling effect on Bogs, a slight rearrangement of King's chronology allows Darabont to attribute Bogs' demise to Hadley's protection of his new investment, a twisting of the source which situates the rooftop showdown a year or so *after* Bogs' beating. In a parodic inversion of the biblical curing of the lame, *The Shawshank Redemption* credits Andy's influence with the crippling of his enemy, who 'never walked again', freeing Dufresne finally (and entirely) from the clutches of The Sisters. By the time Andy comes out of the infirmary, the men for whom he once provided blessed beer have gathered enough chesspiece-sized carvable rocks 'to keep him busy till Rapture', another unusually biblical turn of phrase which again accentuates the undertones of deliverance that are gathering like a storm.

Also awaiting Andy in his cell is the beaming form of Rita Hayworth, the poster through which he will step to freedom, shedding the purgatory of Shawshank prison and escaping, quite literally, into the sanctity of the silver screen. It is an image of cinema as a sacred medium for a secular world, susbsuming Christian iconography, and offering a rebellious alternative religion whose visual fantasy will ultimately triumph over the corruption of the material world.

2 The Ass and the Angel:
Raquel Welch vs. Richard Nixon

Perhaps the greatest innovation of Frank Darabont's screenplay
adaptation of Stephen King's novella *Rita Hayworth and Shawshank
Redemption* is the creation of the sublimely demonic figure of Warden
Norton, a compression of three separate characters from the original
source, none of whom possess the hellish majesty which Bob Gunton
brings to life on screen. In King's source, Warden Norton does not enter
the story until the 60s, replacing the physical brutality of his predecessor
Greg Stammas' regime (which ended in 1959) with a more insidious
psychological terror born of thirty years in the bosom of the Baptist
Advent Church of Eliot. Described by Red as 'Jesus-shouting son of a
whore',[33] Norton emerges from the novella as a bigoted religious fanatic
who was 'the foulest hypocrite that I ever saw in a high position'.[34] To this,
Darabont's screenplay directions add that Norton is 'a colorless man in a
gray suit … [with] flinty eyes … [who] looks like he could piss ice water'.[35]
But it is only when Bob Gunton steps before the camera in *The Shawshank*

Preparing a scene in the dining hall

Redemption, his hair cropped and slicked, his eyes narrowed and mean, his jaw set in a tooth-grinding expression which accentuates whatever jowliness his features may naturally possess, that we suddenly recognise Warden Norton for what he truly is: the reincarnation of Richard Milhous Nixon.

Significantly, in King's source, the period of Andy's imprisonment lasts from 1947 (when he is arrested for murder) to 1975 (when he escapes from Shawshank), a period which eerily matches the political career of Nixon, who became a Republican representative in 1947, and who resigned in disgrace from the presidency in 1974. Indeed, casual references to Nixon abound throughout King's *Different Seasons*, from Red's surmising that Andy had actually dug out of his cell 'by the time Nixon was sworn in for his second term' but couldn't escape until after his presidential resignation,[36] to the Afterword jokes about Pat Nixon writing articles about her husband entitled 'I Say He's a Wonderful Guy'.[37] Accordingly, Darabont's adaptation presents Norton frequently in political-address mode, with scenes such as his announcement of the roof re-tarring project depicting him as an accomplished and confident public speaker.

More important, however, is the sanctimonious manner in which he addresses the servile masses, posing as a decent, holy man while running the kind of corrupt scams for which Nixon would become infamous – 'obstruction of justice' and 'abuse of power' being just two of the impeachment articles recommended by the House Judiciary Committee in 1974. Most striking in this context is Norton's announcement of the 'Inside Out programme', which is located in King's novella as sometime around 1960 ('sixteen or seventeen years' prior to Red's manuscript date, which flickers inconsistently between 1976 and 1977) but which Darabont specifically and pointedly relocates to 1963 – 'the year Kennedy was shot'. His choice of this as the year in which Norton's corruption breaks out of the prison and into the community seems particularly pointed, since JFK defeated Nixon in 1960 only to be assassinated three years later, signalling the end of the dream of 'honest politics'.

As the camera sweeps over the brimmed hats of the assembled press, scribbling and snapping at the Warden's every word, Norton is revealed standing in podiumed splendour before the walls of Shawshank Prison, the vast gothic form of Mansfield Reformatory looming behind him like the lair of some vampiric Count. 'No free ride,' drones Norton, in familiarly deceitful tones, 'but rather a genuine progressive advance in corrections and rehabilitation' which provides slave labour 'at a bare minimum of expense to Mr and Mrs John Q Taxpayer'. Watch Gunton's reassuringly mannered hand movements and slyly lying smile as he uses words like 'properly supervised', 'honest day's labour' and 'valuable service to the community' and you can sense the ghost of Nixon's notorious 'Checkers' address (in which he dismissed charges of financial misdealings with quips about his dog) wafting eerily over the airways. Similarly, when he later accepts a bribe in a cake-box and tells his old friend Ed to 'be sure and thank Maisie for this fine pie', you almost expect him to go on and compliment her on her 'respectable Republican cloth coat', as Nixon complimented his wife in his address.

Although Norton makes a few early appearances in Darabont's film, it is not until his first cell-bound encounter with Andy Dufresne (in the wake of the cinematic miracle of *Gilda*) that he becomes a genuine

Norton (Bob Gunton) takes direction on his licence-plate factory address

Bob Gunton as Samuel Norton/Richard Nixon

presence, sweeping imperiously through the prison corridors, picking cells to be tossed ('one nineteen, one twenty-three') like the chapters from the Bible which he quotes with such ingenuity. When the wardens arrive (in the manner of a Roman guard) at the doors of Dufresne's cell, Andy is duly discovered reading his copy of the good book, to which he holds firm as his cell is casually trashed. Finally coming face to face with Andy, Norton glowers with satisfaction at the Bible before entering into a game of New Testament quotations, fondling the book but failing to open it and look inside its pages – an oversight which has disastrous consequences, both literal and metaphorical.

'Watch ye therefore,' quotes Andy from the Gospel of Mark in sardonic fashion, 'for ye know not when the master of the house cometh,' a sly ribbing of his adversary, who seems grimly amused by his impertinence. 'Always liked that one,' leers Norton. 'But I prefer "I am the light of the world. He that followeth me shall not walk in darkness. But shall have the light of life."' The selection of this passage from John has significance beyond the sheer hubris with which Norton seems to identify himself as Andy's saviour, an idolatrous, material God to be meekly followed on the road to hell. For in apparently identifying himself as 'the light of the world', Norton also (accidentally?) invokes the spectre of Lucifer, the bearer of light, with whom he seems rather more closely acquainted. Sometime later, when taunting the imprisoned Andy in the darkness of solitary confinement, Norton is again depicted as a source of light, Andy averting his eyes from the painful glare as the Warden threatens to cast him 'down with the sodomites', and (again accidentally?) describes himself as a kind of neo-Hitler, presiding over a fiery bonfire of books. 'They'll see the flames for miles,' he drools, adding with a smile, 'We'll dance around it like Indians …' (There are echoes here, too, of Michael Reeves' *Witchfinder General* or Ken Russell's *The Devils*, with the inquisitorial Norton exacting hideous sexualised tortures in the name of the Bible.)

When Andy correctly identifies Norton's quotation as John 8: 12, the Warden immediately transforms his quiet scriptural literacy into the basest of usury tricks, announcing that Andy 'is good with numbers', reducing his Bible to the level of an accountant's ledger. (The unnoticed replacement of Norton's own ledger with Andy's Bible will later provide an excellently irreverent punch-line to this exchange.) Moments later, glancing at the poster of the beaming Rita Hayworth, Norton significantly fails to notice the word 'MOTHER' scratched in the wall above the image, and again his short-sightedness fails on two levels. On a physical level, Norton completely overlooks the possibility that a wall that can be scratched may also be breached, thereby ignoring the gaping hole which is presumably already being made behind the figure of 'lovely Rita'. Symbolically, as a man for whom 'Christianity' is ironically a closed book, Norton also misinterprets Andy's interest in Hayworth as entirely sexual,

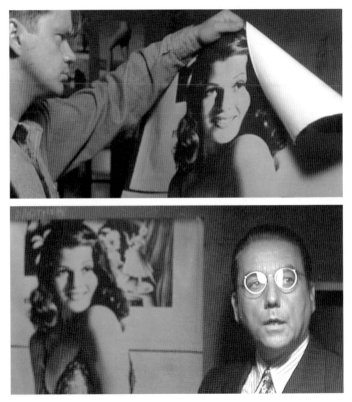

Andy meets Rita; Rita baffles Norton

failing to connect her image with the written word 'MOTHER', and thus missing the indication that she may be serving a purpose closer to that of the Virgin Mary than the Whore of Babylon, acting as an intermediary between Andy and his dreams of cinematic heaven. So deliberate, in fact, seems the juxtaposition of the poster and the word that one may be inclined to believe that Darabont has consciously constructed it as a makeshift shrine, an icon of cinema's own Madonna through whose intercessory powers celluloid redemption is ultimately offered.

When Norton almost walks off with Andy's Bible, he completes an unholy trilogy of godforsaken errors which will characterise his relationship with his as yet unrecognised vanquisher. Passing the book back through the bars of Dufresne's cell, Norton tells Andy, 'Salvation lies within', another religious proclamation whose innate truth he utterly fails to appreciate. For Andy, salvation does indeed lie within: within his *soul*, where the strength and determination to survive are growing stronger every day; within his *cell*, where the hole which will lead him to freedom is getting larger every night; and within his *Bible*, the pages of which have been hollowed out to hide the rock hammer with which he is chiselling his way to freedom, and which Norton now hands back to him with a smug, sanctimonious smile. If, as some believe, evil is indeed the crucible of good, then Warden Samuel Norton is here depicted as a most excellent emissary (or embodiment) of the devil, helping Andy on the road to redemption even as he attempts to corrupt and confuse him.

The rapidity with which Norton's nominally evil actions begin to have an invigorating effect upon Andy is startling indeed. Although his reassignment to library duties is swiftly revealed as a scam to exploit Andy's business acumen, the subsequent interaction with prison guards who approach him as clients rather than jailers swiftly restores whatever sense of self-respect Dufresne may have had in his former life as a banker. A politely removed hat and a handshake from Dekins (which almost causes Brooks Hatlen to soil himself) are just the first in a line of apparently minor gestures which radically redefine the nature of Andy's existence, giving him back the name ('Mister Dufresne') and status which he enjoyed in the pre-fall Eden of his former life.

East of Eden

It is at around this time, as Andy steadily builds the Shawshank Prison Library into a veritable seat of learning, that something unimaginable happens: Brooks Hatlen gets parole. In King's novella, Brooks exists only as a figment of Red's imagination, a character who is referred to only in absence as anecdotal proof of the power of institutionalisation. It is Darabont's invention to have Brooks and Andy interact as curators of the library, King merely allowing Dufresne to pick up the reigns of a cushy job *after* Hatlen has been released. In Darabont's screenplay and film, however, Brooks Hatlen becomes a physical presence, effectively embodied by veteran actor James Whitmore, who makes his first appearance during an early breakfast scene, feeding maggots to his pet crow Jake. (Alongside the weighty symbolic parallels of the caged bird whose entrapment has become irreversible, and the allusions to classic prison movies like *The Bird Man of Alcatraz*, 'Jake' is also the focus of one of *Shawshank*'s most popular trivial tales in which the American Humane Association insist that he only be fed maggots which have already 'died of natural causes'.) Although arguably dismissable as an incidental character,

Frank Darabont directs James Whitmore as the released Brooks Hatlen

Frank Darabont directs William Sadler (Heywood) in the Hatlen Library

included and expanded to lend authentic ballast to the drama, Brooks' heartbreaking fate outside the walls of Shawshank Prison in fact serves a greater purpose in the grand scheme of Darabont's tale: to clarify the nature of Red's ultimate redemption, and to make explicit the oddly positive parallels between release and death which haunt *The Shawshank Redemption*.

'These walls are funny,' says Red of Brooks' fifty-year incarceration. 'First you hate 'em, then you get used to them. Enough time passes, you get so you depend on them.' Concluding that Brooks' admittedly pitiful status within the prison had left him 'institutionalised', Red prefigures his own inability to take a piss on the outside without asking for permission, and seems to accept without question that 'they send you here for life, and that's exactly what they take.' Eschewing subtlety or evasion, Darabont now depicts Brooks on the bus to 'freedom' in a shot which echoes Andy's arrival at Shawshank, making clear that Hatlen is doing nothing more than entering the confines of a new prison: the world outside. Shot on and around the streets of Mansfield (which, with its steamy diners and gleaming soda fountains, still looks oddly like a town out of time), the following montage efficiently zips through Brooks' other-worldly travails: feeding pigeons in the park in the vain hope of Jake's return; packing groceries at a store, where his 'easy-peasy Japaneezy' librarian duties are nothing more than a memory; and dreaming an insomniac's dream of killing his employer so that he may be sent 'home' to Shawshank.

A more purgatorial existence one cannot imagine; trapped between the unsatisfyingly vague comforts of the free man's material world and the terrifyingly real horrors of a life without purpose or direction. Effectively abandoned, Brooks seems condemned to live out his days in limbo, existing neither in heaven nor hell, but in the uncomfortable twilight zone of the eternally lost soul. When Hatlen opts to 'check out', taking his own life in a gesture which seems finally to complete the plan initiated by the prison authorities, it is possible to interpret his death as the ultimate admission of failure. But Brooks is crucially *not* a character in his own right. No matter how much Darabont and Whitmore may flesh out his

Brooks, Andy and Red get on the bus

bones, Brooks Hatlen remains a ghost in the machine of *The Shawshank Redemption*, a cinematic apparition who exists primarily as a warning to those around him, and in particular to Red if he does not follow in the footsteps of Andy Dufresne. Everything about Brooks' release and demise will be mirrored in Red's own last journey, from the awkward moments at the store checkout, to the wooden beam bars of the halfway house through which the camera peers as Brooks prepares to escape his life. 'Brooks was here', he begins to carve above the rafter from which he will hang. 'So was Red' will come the reply. The only difference being the place to which each will *go* from here.

Brooks and Red, lost on the streets of Mansfield

And God Created Man (and Man Created Movies)

From the mock-Christian burial of Jake the 'instutionalised' bird, which Andy suggests in Darabont's script (but not the finished film), to the playing of *The Marriage of Figaro* on the prison PA, for which he gets thrown into solitary, Andy Dufresne now begins to take an increasingly priestly role within Shawshank, ministering directly to the spiritual needs of his fellow inmates while fiddling the money for his godless jailers. Emphasising the 'doubling' motif (a handy screen shorthand for the routine of prison life), Red's second parole hearing is a virtual rerun of the first, as he again invokes 'God's honest truth' in his pat plea of being a reformed character, and is again REJECTED for early release, a stamp which

Brooks and Red preparing to 'check out'

is seen as an ironic blessing in the wake of Hatlen's suicide. As a consolation prize, Andy (who has now been in Shawshank for a decade) gives Red a harmonica, which he receives with the affection of a love token, but which he declines to play – for the moment at least. Later, a brief shot of Red in his cell tentatively breathing into the harmonica before giving up the ghost ('didn't make much sense in here', he says earlier) suggests perhaps a dawning awareness of hope, the *possibility* at least of music in a world deafened by the clanging of prison bars.

According to Darabont's screenplay directions for this scene, '[Red] considers trying it out – even holds it briefly to his lips, almost embarrassed – but puts it back in its box untested. And there the harmonica will stay …'[38] This, indeed, is the last we see of Red's harmonica, although according to one key member of the production team, it almost made a significant appearance in what became the film's closing coda. Struggling to solve the problem of depicting Zihuatanejo in a manner which sufficiently captured its other-worldly significance, Darabont apparently toyed with the idea of having Morgan Freeman finally play the harmonica as he strolled up the beach toward Andy in the closing shots of *The Shawshank Redemption* – confirming the escapist virtues of music established in the *Marriage of Figaro* sequence. As things stand, Freeman's cell-bound failure of faith produces a fade-to-black which is then broken by a hammer smashing through a wall, prefiguring

'Brooks was here': Hatlen is trapped behind the bars of freedom

Andy's ultimate escape, but also symbolically linking Dufresne's victory
with the breakdown of Red's own institutionalised hopelessness.

With the poster of Rita Hayworth now replaced by the classic image
of Marilyn Monroe standing over the air vent in *The Seven Year Itch*
(Robbins stares up at her in Christ-like pose, eyes wide open in awe),
Andy achieves a minor miracle in Shawshank, symbolically raising Brooks
Hatlen from the dead in the form of a memorial library which soon
becomes 'the best prison library in New England'. Meanwhile, as the
prisoners benefit from Andy's higher education, Norton uses his financial
skills to cook the books, laundering the ill-gotten proceeds of his devious
business ventures, which he stashes in a safe behind an embroidered

Andy's light breaks the darkness surrounding Red

inscription made by his wife in church, bearing the legend 'His Judgement Cometh and that Right Soon'. In King's novella, Red offers the pointedly humorous observation that most of the prisoners in Shawshank 'felt that judgment had already occurred',[39] that they were now beyond the land of the living, a theme which is further explored in Darabont's film. It is significant too that while Norton hides his own safe behind a picture ('His Judgement Cometh'), he fails to imagine that Andy may be doing something similar. When Roger Deakins's camera peers *out* of Norton's safe to see the Warden making a deposit, we are being primed for a later shot in which we are invited to stare out of the tunnel through which Andy has escaped, leaving Norton staring blankly into the abyss.

Andy worships at the shrine of Marilyn Monroe

The miracles come to a head in a conversation between Andy and Red in which Dufresne reveals the full extent of his involvement in Norton's money-laundering business. Shot through the shelves of the bookcases which now fill the Brooks Hatlen library, this low-key conversation finds Red listening in amazement as Andy admits his greatest achievement:the creation of a man whom he has conjured 'out of thin air'. 'You can't just make a person up,' says Red, bewildered, to which Andy replies blithely, 'Sure you can.' And indeed he has, in the person of Randall Stephens (Peter Stevens in both novella and screenplay), executor of a number of bank accounts through which the profits of Warden Norton's scams must pass. As yet, Randall exists only on paper, 'a phantom;

Norton seen from the black hole of his safe, and from the abyss of Andy's escape tunnel an apparition; second cousin to Harvey the Rabbit'. Yet in this purgatorial netherworld in which the material universe seems already to have passed away (and in which movies like *Harvey* offer more chance of escape than parole boards), Randall Stephens is as real as Red, Heywood or any of the other inmates – indeed, in many respects he is *more* real, and certainly more *rich*. In terms which have any meaning in the Shawshank universe, Andy appears to have become some sort of god, the writer/director of his own movie, the creator of a fictional character whom we shall eventually meet on screen, and who will ultimately whisk him over the border to Mexico.

The Only Innocent Man in Shawshank

The repetitions increase as Tommy Williams arrives in 1965, his introduction via a tracking shot down the aisle of the prison bus mimicking Andy's arrival, with Dufresne himself now bearing the sagely mantle of wise old lag, greying of hair and paternal of nature. But the Shawshank into which Williams is inducted is notably different from that which greeted Andy back in 1947. Now fitted with a handsome library through which Andy has 'helped a dozen guys get their high-school diploma' (again, the possibly significant use of 'a dozen' – twelve men who have followed Andy's lead), it has become a place in which a young innocent like Tommy is able (at least initially) to thrive and learn, rather than suffer and submit. This time there is no suggestion of Red and his cohorts taking bets on which new fish will crack first – instead, we see them laughing, working and chatting together, while Red's noticeably cheerier voice-over informs us that 'We liked [Tommy] immediately.' When Andy is aggressively asked what he's doing time for, he pauses only momentarily before quoting Heywood's phrase 'Lawyer fucked me', and then adding, as laughter breaks out around the table, 'Everybody's innocent in here, didn't you know that?' And this time the laughter seems not hollow, but joyous.

Bristling with naive charm, Tommy becomes Andy's 'new project' as he resolves to help him through his high-school equivalency tests, thereby hopefully nudging him back toward 'rehabilitation'. In Andy's cell, we see

the product of nearly twenty years' incarceration, the polished stones on the window-sill giving way to an entire chessboard of carvings, the now full-colour image of a fur-bikinied Raquel Welch in *One Million Years BC* covering the *real* work to which Andy has been devoting his free time. When Tommy storms out of his exams in 1966, binning his paper with a dismissive 'fuck this place!', it is Andy who quietly retrieves his efforts from the trash and sends them in for official appraisal, and ultimate reward.

And it is only now, nearly ninety minutes into the movie, that the issue of Andy's guilt of the crime of which he is convicted is finally called into question. Unlike King's novella, which reveals as early as its fourth page that Dufresne was one of 'less than ten men' that Red believed innocent, Darabont makes us wait until Tommy's cataclysmic revelation before allowing Andy's opening courtroom pleas to bear any weight whatsoever. Indeed, even in the moment *immediately* prior to Tommy's announcement that he shared a cell with the *real* killer, Red – the person who knows (and loves) Andy more than anyone else in the world – declares stoically that Andy 'caught his wife in bed with some golf pro; greased 'em both'. His certainty is absolute; his acceptance infinite.

While the subsequent shenanigans surrounding Tommy's tales of Elmo Blatch have enormous narrative import (in both novella and film), what is most notable about them is the relatively minor impact they have on the underlying subtext of the story. For although Tommy's memories of

From Rita to Marilyn to Raquel: Andy's latest pin-up

Blatch's deranged confessions about murdering Andy's wife and her lover bear out Andy's courtroom insistence of innocence, it is ironically the unabashed acceptance of *guilt* by both Andy *and* Red which will ultimately set them both free. To understand this, we must look ahead to the sequence which follows in the wake of Tommy's demise (in the novella, he is merely transferred rather than murdered by Norton) in which Andy tells Red of his dream of Zihuatanejo. In King's novella, the emphasis in this episode is on Andy's extraordinary ability to plan ahead, as he recounts the burial of a safe-deposit-box key under a piece of volcanic rock in a field in Buxton, the creation of a fictional trustee, Peter Stevens, giving him access to funds on his release (or escape) which would otherwise have been sequestered.

In Darabont's version, however, a far weightier issue is brought into play – the issue of Andy's confession. 'I killed her Red', he tells his friend blankly, an admission which we now know to be materially untrue, but which seems to have resonance beyond the immediate physical facts. A few moments later, when he begins to talk of the hayfield in Buxton, Andy is notably enigmatic about what lies under that rock, stating only (and ominously) that 'there's something buried under it I want you to have …' Whether intentional or not (and I believe it to be so), the implication of this exchange is that what lies under the rock is in fact Andy's gun, famously missing since the first reel of the film, when he claimed to have

The madman laughs: Elmo Blatch reveals the awful truth

thrown it into the Royal River. Indeed, even despite his qualifying proviso that 'I didn't pull the trigger', Andy's confession seems to accept full responsibility for his wife's death, an eventuality which he now sees as a result of his inability to show her love, thereby driving her into the hands of another man.

Although Red misinterprets his friend's words as an outpouring of guilty despair (which on some level they may be), far more significant is the act of absolution which they represent, and which will be swiftly rewarded by Andy's successful escape. In one sense, Andy's 'confession' may be read as an ultimate acceptance of original sin, a pre-communion admission of guilt from which only forgiveness (rather than innocence) can free him. On a subtextual level, this seems to be both significant and deliberate, taking us back the opening of *The Shawshank Redemption* in which Darabont (unlike King) clearly led us to believe that Andy *may* have killed his wife, and reminding us that our acceptance of him has never been predicated on a belief in his infallibility.

Conversely, Warden Norton's response to the possible 'proof' of Andy's innocence is one of spectacular guilt, his patronisingly Nixonian tones quashing the suggestion of conspiracy in infamously familiar fashion. (Think again of Nixon's 'Checkers' address; or his televised dismissal of allegations regarding the Watergate bugging.) In a marvellously compact movement, editor Richard Francis-Bruce cuts from Elmo Blatch's cackling cell-bound narrative (a story within a story within a story) to a two-shot from behind Tommy's head, Andy's eyes widening in horror and hope, to a close-up of a shirt-sleeved, implacable Norton, his granite-faced expression worthy of a politician cornered during a television interview. (The impression of Andy being caught between *two* madmen, Blatch and Norton, is heightened by the doubling of an editing device which previously allowed Red's narrative voice-over to segue straight into Norton's speech as he announced the licence-factory project, and here allowing Tommy's revelatory tale to railroad straight into Blatch's ramblings: two narrators, two villains, one stylistic tick.) As for Norton's unflinching stonewalling of Tommy's revelations – that his story wasn't true, and even if it *was* it would make no difference

Norton/Judas signals Hadley to kill Tommy

– the spin-doctors of Washington could scarcely do better. As Andy, the awakening innocent, asks in awe-struck incredulity: 'How can you be so *obtuse …?*'

From obtuse to obstreperous, Norton's reactions to Andy's outburst take *The Shawshank Redemption* to new heights of melodrama, as Andy faces a month of solitary confinement, and Tommy is casually murdered on the Warden's orders. Summoned to a late-night assignation with Norton, the recently diploma'd (but still none too bright) Tommy is suckered in by the kind of parodically cornball dialogue which the voting public so often mistake for sincerity: 'I tell you son,' says Norton in mock-paternal fashion, 'this thing really came along and knocked my wind out. It's got me up nights, and that's the truth.' Attentive viewers will notice an echo in Norton's words of Red's previous parole-hearing pleas ('that's the God's honest truth') and may be inclined to see both speeches as nothing more than contemptuous performances. As Norton reaches out to pat Tommy on the shoulder, invoking the biblical justice of 'Almighty God himself', we are offered a momentary flash of Judas in the Garden of Gethsemane signalling the Roman soldiers to move in. 'The right thing to do,' says Norton. 'Sometimes it's hard to know what that is.' A moment later, Hadley guns Tommy down, leaving him lying face down in the dirt, his corpse illuminated by a prison light; Lucifer's radiance shrouded in darkness.

Andy cowers from Norton's Luciferian light

The Road to Zihuatanejo

Despite his impending death, the news of Tommy's exam success nonetheless pierces the armour of despair which now surrounds Andy in solitary. The merest flicker of a smile which plays over his decaying features as he huddles in a dark, painful corner suggests some form of spiritual sustenance, an internal boost akin to that previously attributed to the work of 'Mr Mozart'. Like the base metal transformed into gold by an act of alchemy, Tommy has briefly become a magical talisman for Andy, slipping from fecklessness to self-awareness, sinner to martyr. Under such circumstances, not even Norton's murderous scheming, nor his threats to turn Andy over to The Sisters ('You'll think you've been fucked by a train …') can entirely obliterate his sense of resolution in the face of defeat. We *know* that the drama is moving toward a climax, for which Tommy's death is but the catalyst. And although the emotional signposts seem to point toward suicide, the narrative arc is clearly leading us to the foot of an altogether more miraculous rainbow. (Interestingly, a more despairing episode is offered in King's novella, in which Tommy is not murdered by Norton, but simply bought off – transferred to a minimum security prison in return for his silence.)

'I was in the path of the tornado,' Andy tells Red. 'I just didn't expect the storm would last as long as it has.' And now we come to most explicitly transcendental passage in both novel and film: Andy's description of Zihuatanejo, a Mexican town on the shores of the Pacific Ocean to which he escapes in his dreams. 'You know what the Mexicans say about the Pacific?' asks Andy enigmatically. 'They say it has no memory. That's where I want to live the rest of my life – a warm place with memory.' As we noted earlier, the concept of 'memory' (or the lack of it) is of crucial importance to Red's tale of Andy Dufresne, intertwined with the concepts of guilt and innocence with which the narrative wrestles. In the opening scenes of Darabont's movie, Andy is heard to proclaim in court that 'I really don't remember' some of the key details of the night of his wife's death, a plea which seems to be deliberately evasive, hinting at hidden guilt. In King's novella, the purchase of dishtowels used to muzzle and silence a gun becomes a key element in the prosecution of Andy, with a store clerk clearly remembering that he had bought them, while Andy 'couldn't remember *not* buying them'.[40]

The reason for this discrepancy, in Andy's summation, is that 'memory is such a *goddam* subjective thing',[41] an appraisal which has particular significance for King's narrator who is, in the end, offering nothing more than his own '*goddam* subjective' remembrance of his friend. In King's written source, Andy is – quite literally – nothing more than a memory, a subtle differentiation from Darabont's screen adaptation in which, by the very nature of the medium, we seem to meet Dufresne in person. Yet in Andy's description of Zihuatanejo, the absence of memory as a form of absolution remains constant from page to screen, a talismanic evocation of a state of being in which the sins of the past are washed away by the waters of the Pacific Ocean – whose name, significantly, means 'peace'. In both versions, it is clear that Andy is describing a utopian environment in which the tribulations of his former life will cease to exist; a vision of paradise by another name. But it is Darabont (rather than King) who positions this speech immediately after Andy's admission of guilt, reinforcing the suggestion that Zihuatanejo only becomes a reality in the wake of confession.

Interestingly, although some Christian viewers have chosen to interpret Zihuatanejo as a vision of heaven in which all sins are forgotten, it *is* also possible to read the absence of memory as a profoundly Nietzschean state of guiltlessness, in which we have moved *beyond* the traditional dynamic of good and evil, and outside of the realms of religious values and oppositions. For Nietzsche, forgetting was a typically *a*-Christian virtue, representing the obliteration (rather than the forgiveness) of 'sin'. In such an interpretation, absolute amnesia may ironically represent the *absence* (rather than the presence) of divinity (Nietzsche's God is dead), thus making it possible to read Andy's longing for 'a place that has no memory' as entirely secular and atheistic. Rather than being a Christ-figure, Andy may be read more as a Zarathustra-like prophet, offering (unlike the sanctimonious Norton) a radical model of escape (or self-overcoming) through education and the experience of freedom, while Red finds himself still tied to the traditional model of crime and punishment.

In his FilmFour *Viewfinder* interview, Tim Robbins speculated about the meaning of 'Zihuatanejo', and concluded that it was an idea which somehow made universal a drama which may otherwise have held limited appeal:

In the end, it's a film about people being in jail and having hope to get out of that jail. Now, why is that universal? Not everybody has been in jail. But maybe on a deeper level, a metaphysical level, people feel enslaved by their environments, their jobs, their relationships, by whatever it is in the course of their lives that puts the wall or the bars around them. And the idea that you can survive for many, many years in this kind of enslavement, or prison of your own making, and that there's a Zihuatanejo somewhere in your future – I think that's something that really is important to people; the idea that Zihuatanejo can exist for all of us.[42]

While Robbins is specifically *not* speaking from a religious standpoint, there is a significant crossover between his secular interpretation of Zihuatanejo as an embodiment of amorphous hope, and that offered by the Christian fans of Darabont's movie featured in Russell Leven and Andrew Abbott's documentary *Shawshank: The Redeeming Feature* who see it as a specific metaphor for paradise regained. Crucially, in *neither* interpretation does the actual earthly town of Zihuatanejo (where Robbins has joked he should open a bar called 'Andy & Red's') play *any* significant role beyond the metaphorical; but in both, the idea of transcending the tortures of the world seems tangible. When Red talks of his own inability to embrace the idea of Zihuatanejo (as he does in both King's novella and Darabont's film), it is clear that his description of his own institutionalisation is also a description of the absence of hope which now keeps him imprisoned. To him, Mexico and the Pacific Ocean are nothing more than 'shitty pipe dreams', a memorable line from *The Shawshank Redemption* which playfully rejigs Stephen King's description of 'pipedreams in a shitty little prison exercise yard'[43] into a pun-laden prefiguring of Andy's imminent death and rebirth in the sewage pipes of Shawshank Prison.

Real to Reel: Andy's Ascension

'Lord, it's a miracle!' screams Warden Norton with enraged, exasperated irony as the tomb of Andy's prison cell is found to conceal not a lifeless body, but a spectacularly lively absence. And miraculous it certainly appears to be, both to Norton *and* to the audience, particularly since the events immediately prior to Andy's escape have deliberately signalled suicide as a possibility, even an inevitability. Having listened to Andy's wide-eyed stories of Zihuatanejo, Red tells his fellow inmates that Dufresne is cracking up, an assessment ominously reinforced by Heywood's tales of acquiring for him a 6 foot length of rope. (Brooks Hatlen has already hung himself in *The Shawshank Redemption*, and Red will later be seen making preparations which exactly mirror his demise.)

It is in the wake of this morbid conversation that Dufresne is seen for the last time ministering to the corrupt needs of Warden Norton, polishing the dead man's shoes into which he will step (literally) as he sheds his worldly skin and becomes the 'phantom' of his own imagination. In these shoes he will be seen 'walking Spanish' down the halls of Shawshank Prison, shuffling toward his cell like a condemned man moving toward the gallows, observed by Red, whose premonitions of death cause him to endure his 'longest night' in stir. When Andy fails to exit his cell at parade-call the next morning, the guard's threat that 'you better be sick or dead in there' has a deliberately hollow ring about it, the spectre of suicide hanging in the silence. But the look of wonder and bewilderment which fills the guard's face as he peers into Cell 245 indicates something far more mysterious (this is a tale by Stephen King after all), an apparently supernatural eventuality encapsulated by his awed exclamation: '*Oh my Holy God!*'

Now, events escalate rapidly, as we cut to Norton discovering Andy's raggedy shoes, abandoned like the shed skin of a reborn snake, and charging to the cell where his prisoner 'just wasn't here'. Overcome with disbelief (a strangely appropriate state for such a hypocritical religious zealot), Norton throws his hands into the air in pantomime parody of an evangelist in the throes of ecstatic revelation and commits the very crime he first told the inmates he would *not* tolerate in Shawshank: blasphemy. With a final flourish of ironically Nixonian dialogue ('this is a *conspiracy* ...

and *everyone's in on it ...* including *her!*'), Norton suffers a moment of damning inspiration and hurls a rock toward the poster of Raquel, whose wild-haired form dominates one wall of Andy's cell, and into whose world of escapist celluloid fantasy the rock promptly disappears ...

'I once asked [Andy] what the posters meant to him,' remembers Red in King's source novella, to which Dufresne replies simply,

Freedom. You look at those pretty women and you feel like you could almost ... not quite but *almost* step right through and be beside them ... Didn't you ever feel that way about a picture, Red? That you could almost step right through it?' ... Years later I saw exactly what he meant ...[44]

Now, as Roger Deakins' camera tracks down the chiselled tunnel that has led Andy to freedom, we too understand these words: that Andy has indeed stepped through the image of *One Million Years BC*, and joined Raquel on the sands of Zihuatanejo, a paradise defined by a peculiar mixture of trash movies and archaic religion. (There is significance, too, in the fact that in a film almost totally devoid of women, save for their luminous cinematic images, it is a dead wife who first gets Andy into this mess, and a pin-up – whose glossy image fetishistically conceals a gaping tunnel – who gets him out of it.)

This is the climactic conjunction of the story's 'church of the cinema' subtext, a physical depiction of film's miraculous ability to

The ass and the angel: Norton tears down Raquel

transport the viewer from the grey confines of the here and now into the endless possibilities of visual fantasy. In this context, Darabont's alteration of the poster through which Dufresne steps is of particular import, with the Linda Ronstadt of King's source ('looking back over her shoulder, her hands tucked into the back pockets of a very tight pair of fawn-colored slacks'[45]) being replaced by Raquel Welch, who makes a 'record-breaking' but crucially not *headlining* appearance in *Rita Hayworth and Shawshank Redemption*. It is, indeed, slightly unusual that of *all* the pin-ups cited in King's source, only Ronstadt lacks a cinematic connection, and yet it is *her* image through which Dufresne ultimately escapes – perhaps country rock music holds a greater significance for King than cinema, but not (it seems) for Darabont.

The Arsehole of the World

From the sublime to the ridiculous, King's novel and Darabont's shooting script now include an oddly humorous episode in which a guard traces Andy's movements through the hole and down toward the broken sewage pipe, where he promptly pukes his guts up ('It's shit! Oh my God it's shit!'[46]) while Red laughs like a drunken hyena. (The tunnel, incidentally,

Andy's escape hits the newsstands

stills resides in the halls of Mansfield Reformatory, as indeed does the 'shitty pipe' – props from the movie which have now become revered relics for fans of *The Shawshank Redemption.*) In his screenplay notes, Darabont mourns the dropping of this scene, which ultimately *'didn't belong in the movie'*,[47] and talks affectionately of the footage of Morgan Freeman in paroxysms of delight. 'It was probably the most memorable scene for me,' confirmed Freeman later. 'They'd sent a young guard down to the hole that Andy went through, and he didn't like it *at all.* And Red's just listening to him screaming up through the hole, and laughing ... I mean *laughing.* So I had to laugh for what seemed like for ever ...'[48]

With the laughter gone, the narrative now spirals back through the passage of time to discover Andy stumbling upon the seeds of his salvation as he first carved the letter A on the wall of his cell nearly twenty years earlier. As the cement fragments around his rock hammer, Andy is seen in montage depositing rock debris in the exercise yard, in the manner of the industrious tunnellers from the classic POW movie *The Great Escape.* From here, we hurry forward again to Andy's last night in prison (on earth?) as he packs his chess set and Norton's clothes and accountant's ledger, then says a silent prayer before crawling into Raquel's world, and down toward the sewage drain. Evoking another film fantasy classic, Darabont nods his head toward the iconography of James Whale's *Frankenstein* (and also, I suspect, toward Mel Brooks' *Young Frankenstein*)

'It's alive!' Andy as Frankenstein

with lightning crashing about Andy's head, a look of wild-eyed madness on his face which seems to cry 'It's alive!' as he uses the storm to help him secretly break out of Shawshank.

It is with an admirable devotion to King's source novella that Darabont now completes the symbolic cycle by having Andy crawl to freedom through 'five hundred yards of shit-smelling foulness' – the Shawshank prison sewage pipe. Seen crawling and puking his way through a river of excremental filth, Andy finally bursts turd-like into the toilet-waters of a creek beyond the perimeter walls of Shawshank, covered from head to foot in the very putrescence of the shit-hole in which he has lived for the past two decades. From a prison in which anal rape was once the

Andy is reborn in the baptismal waters of the creek

order of the day, Andy now commits the most extraordinary act of escapology, literally bursting out of Shawshank's rectum to be reborn again in the cleansing waters of a new world.

The iconic image of Andy Dufresne, stripped to the waist, arms held out in crucified triumph, is created within these waters; it is an image which has become emblematic of *The Shawshank Redemption*, although ironically the film poster uses not a still but a mock-up re-creation of this scene with a faceless model doubling for Robbins. While this image clearly could not feature in King's source (in which Red merely wonders about the actual events of Andy's escape), it is described in detail in Darabont's shooting script in a manner which suggests that the writer/director knew exactly what he wanted. According to the instructions for scene 251:

Andy's face looms from the darkness, peering out at freedom … and plunges head-first into the creek. He comes up sputtering for breath. The water is waist-deep. He wades upstream, ripping his clothes from his body. He gets his shirt off … flings the shirt away. He raises his arms to the sky, turning slowly, feeling the rain washing him clean. Exultant. Triumphant. A FLASH OF LIGHTNING arcs from horizon to horizon.[49]

The effect Darabont is seeking to create is clearly one of transcendent wonderment, an image of a man finally freed from the horrors of his earthly shackles, offering himself up to the heavens.

Unsurprisingly, the filming of this uplifting scene was rather more down-to-earth. According to several sources, the muddy creek into which Tim Robbins actually falls in this sequence was tested for chemicals – a standard precaution in farming areas – and found to be less than fit for human consumption (a local chemist described it as 'lethal'). As Robbins later told me:

The thing is, when you're doing a film, you want to be a good soldier – you don't want to be the one that gets in the way. So you *will* do things as an actor that are compromising to your physical health and safety. I remember thinking 'What are they going to drop me in? This river, or stream or whatever

– *what* is it full of?' And I think I remember asking that I have a shower ready when I finished doing this thing. Big star demands, huh? Just a hot shower. Please.[50]

'His Judgement Cometh and that Right Soon'

Now in the Maine National Bank, slicked and tailored, the phantom Randall Stephens becomes an on-screen reality, an identity created by Andy in which to play out his cinematic dreams, now wealthy to the tune of $370,000. Incidentally, although the figure cited is the same, the source of the money in King's novella has nothing to do with Norton's corrupt dealings, but with Andy's own investments in the name of Peter Stevens

'His Judgement Cometh': Norton discovers Andy's Bible

immediately prior to his conviction. Moreover, in the novella Andy simply breaks out of Shawshank never to be seen again, with Norton suffering nothing worse than humiliating resignation in the wake of Dufresne's jailbreak. In Darabont's adaptation, however, there is an issue of vengeance to be dealt with, and it is with some relish that the writer/director now addresses himself to the events of Norton's downfall.

As the Warden's corrupt business ledgers, which Andy pilfered and posted, are opened, examined and published by the offices of the *Daily Bugle*, the police raid Shawshank Prison, Norton's eyes moving from the arriving cavalcade to the embroidered inscription on his wall, the truth of which he is only now beginning to understand. In a sucker-punch of terrifically irreverent humour, Norton scrabbles into his safe, where he discovers that his accountant's book has been replaced by Andy's Bible ('I hear you're good with numbers'), two sacred volumes which crucially looked exactly the same to the spiritually blind Norton. Opening the leather-bound cover, we see Andy's handwritten inscription: 'Dear Warden. You were right. Salvation lay within' – providing a moment of mock-sanctimonious reverence before the true 'salvation' is revealed in the form of pages hollowed out in the shape of a rock hammer. As the camera watches Norton's crumbling features (a splendid example of facial underacting from Bob Gunton), we remember how he handed that very Bible back to Andy in his cell during their first face-to-face encounter, and

Norton faces his own damnation

wonder whether it already held the tool of his destruction. Moments later, Norton is dead, victim of the same suicidal urge which we had been led to believe was ready to claim Andy. Indeed, in some senses, both Norton and Andy *have* died, gone to meet their respective makers – the latter, to the heaven of Zihuatanejo, the former, to the hell of ignominious self-destruction.

Life after Death

Although Andy has left Shawshank, his presence continues to be felt, kept alive in the laughing recollections of his former friends, whose lives seem to have been transformed by his adventures, and who now live through the stories of his escapades. As for Red, the blank postcard he receives from Fort Hancock, Texas (McNary in the novella), is taken as a sign that Andy has indeed 'crossed', leading him to dreams of his friend powering an open-top convertible (a 1969 Pontiac, despite the 1966 setting) toward the waters of the Pacific. 'It always makes me laugh,' whispers Red in voice-over. 'Andy Dufresne who crawled through a river of shit and came out clean on the other side.' But freedom has yet to come for Red, the true subject of *The Shawshank Redemption*, who is now seen in morose reverie in the real-life pauper's graveyard by the walls of Mansfield Reformatory, ironically saddened by Andy's escape: 'I guess I just miss my friend.'

In Darabont's screenplay, this sadness mutates into something close to horror during an eerie dream sequence in which Red wakes in his cell to find a poster of Rita Hayworth, from which bursts 'a shaft of holy white light'.[51] Sucked into the void by a violent whirlwind, Red is thrown screaming into the abyss, finding himself finally standing on the shores of the Pacific, utterly alone and insignificant as the camera flies away, his voice pleading pitifully, 'I am terrified. There is no way home.' Seemingly inspired by an earlier passage in King's novella in which Red is taunted by 'cruel' images of 'blue water and white beaches' and has nightmares of an anvil-shaped rock which he is unable to lift,[52] this sequence is described by Darabont as 'my best work in the script', the loss of which 'I regret most … If I could have captured on film what I put down on the page … it might have been sublime.'[53] Certainly, the sublime elements are far from

underplayed in the script, as Red awakens in his cell to peer out of his prison bars at the stars, while his voice-over intones a silent prayer: 'Andy, I know you're in that place. Look at the stars for me just after sunset. Touch the sand ... wade in the water ... and feel free.'[54]

While Darabont attributes the dream scene's demise to the simple rigours of his shooting schedule, its absence allows (or forces) him to cut from the pauper's grave to the familiar prison-barred montage of Red's next parole hearing, the third and final appearance of this now well-established motif. Dipping again into the fragments of King's source, Darabont neatly steals a few lines from the second page of the novella and expands them into a speech which Freeman delivers with the resigned

Andy's disciples remember him with joy, while Red mourns his passing

honesty of a guilty man finally facing up to his own damnation. The result is, in my opinion, Freeman's best scene in the film, the point around which the drama truly pivots, the real moment of 'redemption' promised in the title. It is also a textbook example of an actor using minimal facial expressions and vocal inflections to *maximum* effect, a scene of 'I'm Spartacus!' impact with none of the shouty melodrama beloved of modern movies.

Asked again if his (now forty) years in stir have left him rehabilitated, Red unexpectedly drops the 'God's honest truth' patter of yore, and addresses the question as if for the first time. 'Rehabilitated?' he wonders out loud. 'You know I don't have any idea what that means.' When the parole officer begins to explain, patronisingly, that it means he is 'ready to rejoin society', Red cuts him short, the world-weary resignation rich in his voice as he bristles, 'I know what you *think* it means, sonny … To me it's just a made-up word: a politician's word.' Having only recently parted company with Warden Samuel Norton, second cousin to President Richard Nixon, we understand that this is just about the most contemptuous description possible, the juxtaposition of the words 'rehabilitation' and 'politician' leaving a foul smell hanging in the air, here in the very office in which Norton worked his wickedness, and eventually met his maker.

'Am I sorry for what I did?' Red continues. 'There's not a day goes by I don't feel regret … I look back on the way I was then, a young stupid kid who committed that terrible crime. I want to talk to him, I want to try and talk some sense into him, tell him the way things are. But I can't.' And it is now that the true moment of 'redemption' occurs, as Red finally accepts that he cannot save himself, that *nothing* he can do can atone for the sins of the past. (Incidentally, although oblique in Darabont's film, Red's crime is clarified in King's novella as that of murdering his wife for the insurance money, accidentally killing a neighbour and her son in the process. It's also worth noting that in Morgan Freeman's assessment, 'I don't think it's Red's redemption, it's his *salvation*. The "redemption" is Andy's because he was innocent. You don't redeem your life if you pay the price for whatever you did. You atone. So Red atones, and Andy got redemption.'[55])

Redeemed, released and reborn: Red gets parole

Like Andy in the prison yard, confessing to a crime he did not materially commit, Red seems finally to accept his own unassailable guilt, realising at last that only grace, rather than performance, can set him free. In another echo of the pre-communion act of confession, Red publicly confesses his own unworthiness, expecting nothing in return. 'That kid's long gone,' he says with clarity, 'and this old man is all that's left. I gotta live with that.' Then finally, as if to prove that, for once, reward is not his purpose (Red has talked constantly until now of the profit margins on his various scams) he throws a closing insult toward the parole board. 'Rehabilitated?' he sneers. 'That's just a bullshit word. So you go on and stamp your forms, sonny, and stop wasting my time. Because to tell you the truth, I don't give a shit.'

As the 'APPROVED' stamp comes down on the parole application of Ellis Boyd Redding (a name unique to Darabont's script, not King's novella), we move swiftly to Red's release, a hint of camera-overcranking as he walks out of the prison gates, mirroring the scene in which he strolled toward us across the prison yard just prior to Andy's arrival at Shawshank. And now the echoes and doublings come thick and fast: Red on the bus to 'freedom', evoking the prison-bound arrival of Andy and Tommy; Red in the halfway house, where Hatlen carved the inscription 'Brooks was here' before hanging himself from a wooden beam; Red serving in the town store, where his inability to deal with freedom reminds us again of the institutionalisation which ultimately killed Hatlen. Cementing this theme, Red's voice-over plaintively announces that 'All I do any more is think of ways to break my parole so maybe they'd send me back,' his eyes apparently fixed on a gun in the window of a pawnshop as his words echo Brooks' longing to be sent 'home' to Shawshank. Even as Roger Deakins' camera strays across the rows of handguns toward the compass which will in fact direct Red out of his despair, the spectre of suicide hangs heavy in the air, acknowledged by Red's admission that 'only one thing stops me – a promise I made to Andy'.

It is this promise which finally sends Red to the hayfield in Buxton, where the lump of 'volcanic rock' ominously referred to by Andy does indeed await his discovery. In King's source, Red seeks this hayfield out of curiosity rather than obligation, resisting the urge to re-offend simply out of respect for Andy's achievement, because 'what he needed was just to be free, and if I kicked away what I had, it would be like spitting in the face of everything he had worked so hard to win back.'[56] For Darabont, this curiosity becomes a pilgrimage to which Red has committed himself, a promise which he must not break. In both versions, what Red finds under that rock 'that has no earthly business in a Maine hayfield' is the same: a letter addressed to him from Andy (signed Peter in the novella) encouraging him to go the extra mile, to make a leap of faith, to overcome his fear of freedom and follow him to the shores of Zihuatanejo ('you remember the name of the town, don't you?').

Back in the halfway house, Darabont evokes the spectre of death one last time, as Red finally 'checks out' in an act of faux suicide which echoes the departures of both Andy and Brooks. With Dufresne's words 'Get busy livin' or get busy dying' ringing in his ears, Red relives Hatlen's final moments, the chair he used to hang himself looming ominously into shot as Red puts his possessions in order, and scratches his name on the ceiling beam with a penknife. As Red picks up his suitcase and walks purposefully from the room, the camera pans up to see 'Brooks was here' and 'So was Red' scrawled on the wood, implying that this is the place from which both exited the world in which they had become imprisoned. 'For the second time in my life, I'm guilty of committing a crime,' admits Red, as we see him violating his

Heaven and Hell: Red and Brooks make their exits

parole to purchase a bus-ticket for Fort Hancock, the place where Andy 'crossed', and to which Red is now headed.

Return to Zihuatanejo

'Remember,' writes Andy in his letter in both novella and film, 'hope is a good thing, maybe the best of things, and no good thing ever dies. I will be hoping that this letter finds you, and finds you well.' A few hundred words later, King's source story comes to a close with an echo of those words, as Red – a man who once knew only the safety of institutionalised fear – is spurred on by hope to begin a

long journey whose conclusion is uncertain. I hope Andy is down there. I hope I can make it across the border. I hope to see my friend and shake his hand. I hope the Pacific is as blue as it has been in my dreams. I *hope*.[57]

In Darabont's original screenplay, this ending would be perfectly matched on screen, as Red is seen seated on the bus heading for the border, reciting those same words: 'I hope ... I *hope*.'

'To me, that was the perfect ending for the story,' admits Darabont in *Shawshank: The Redeeming Feature*, 'and therefore by extension the perfect ending for the movie. So that's the way I wrote it.'[58] 'It ended on a note of hope but not fulfilment,'[59] confirms producer Niki Marvin, who

Final shot: how *Shawshank* might have ended

clearly remembers the executive producers at Castle Rock asking Darabont to consider reuniting Red and Andy on screen in the final reel, because *that's* what the audience would *want* to see. 'That would be me,' remembers executive producer Liz Glotzer, who also admits that 'Frank thought it would be pandering to an audience somehow – because it came from me, and I was working for the studio, so it was automatically like a glossy "Hollywood Ending".'[60] In his screenplay notes, Darabont concedes that 'I was skeptical' about this suggestion, but also insists that 'I wasn't convinced Castle Rock was *wrong*. So I wrote the added scene, knowing that if it didn't work on film, I could always leave it out of the movie.'[61]

The added scene in question is a sequence beloved by millions of fans of the movie, but which (in my opinion) has no earthly business being in *The Shawshank Redemption* – a sweeping helicopter shot which cross-fades from the bus to the waters of the Pacific Ocean, and from here to the shores of Zihuatanejo, where a beaming, shoeless Red strolls toward the white-clad form of Andy, earnestly sanding a boat. As the men's eyes meet, their faces break into radiant smiles; and as they walk toward each

DP Roger Deakins and first assistant John Woodward walk through a practice run of the new coda ending (photo: Frank Darabont)

other, the camera flies exultantly heavenward, all ambiguities resolved. While accepting the scene's demonstrable popularity, my objections to its presence are both aesthetic and thematic. On a simple surface level, I resent its cod simplicity, its picture-postcard depiction of a place which should remain both invisible and unimaginable. For, as we have seen, it is not 'Zihuatanejo the town', but 'Zihuatanejo the state of mind' toward which King and Darabont's narrative has been inexorably leading us – a state of 'hope' better encapsulated by Red's enigmatic departure from Mansfield, than by his conclusive arrival in St Croix (which doubles in the film for Zihuatanejo). Worse still, this finale reduces the fantastical possibilities of the narrative, in which escapist myth and cinematic magic are splendidly conjoined, to the level of an oddly down-to-earth climax in which a beach and a boat are the greatest rewards imaginable. Having stepped up to join 'lovely Raquel' in the world of *One Million Years BC*, I would be sorely disappointed to find that this was all fantasy cinema had to offer; surely the escapist imagination which takes flight in the church of the cinema can do better than *this*?

Be thankful for small mercies, however; things could have been much worse. 'You look like a man who knows how to get things,' says Andy in the rewritten shooting script, in a line which was ultimately dropped in favour of ecstatic silence. 'I'm known to locate certain things from time to time,'[62] replies Red, taking off his jacket, and picking up a sander. 'When spoken, these lines … had a cloying "golly-gee-ain't-we-cute" quality that would have sent you screaming from the theater,' writes Darabont, who candidly admits leaving them 'reeking like dog turds on the cutting room floor',[63] but who still feels that the final unspoken encounter at Zihuatanejo is justified:

I shot this little ending on the beach, where we actually *do* see them getting together again. And I thought that after the two hours and twenty minutes of the sort of hell they've been through – this huge emotional experience that we've taken the audience on – we may owe them the catharsis of seeing these men rejoined.[64]

'I just remember getting out of Mansfield!' laughs Tim Robbins. 'Getting out of Mansfield and going to St Croix! It was like "Oh, thank God!" Because it was beautiful down there, and the weather was beautiful. And personally I think you *need* that ending. You *definitely* need that ending ...'[65] Morgan Freeman agrees, insisting that 'that moment of reconnection was very powerful, and I think it gave it a better sense of closure.'[66] This was the conclusion which Darabont himself reached during the test-screenings of *The Shawshank Redemption*, in which audiences 'wept and cheered' and voted the finale their favourite scene in the movie. 'As soon as he saw it, he knew he wanted to use it,' says Liz Glotzer of Castle Rock, who had specifically committed themselves to financing this sequence without requiring its inclusion in the finished film:

We said to him, 'Basically you have final cut. Although it's not in a legal document, we'll give you final cut, we won't make you do *anything* you don't want to do.' And I think that allowed him to feel free to try things. He knew he could shoot it and know that we weren't going to *force* him to put it in the movie.[67]

'[T]here are a few purists in the crowd who would have preferred ending with King's image of the bus going down the road,' admits Darabont gallantly in his notes to the published *Shawshank* screenplay:

[But] there's a difference between pandering to an audience and giving them something they love. Besides, as I said, I'd started falling in love with it myself ... By ending with that final image, we've brought the viewer on a full journey that begins in tight claustrophobia defined by walls and concludes where the horizon is limitless; the movie has traveled fully from darkness to light, from coldness to warmth, from colorlessness to a place where only color exists, from physical and spiritual imprisonment to total freedom ... Bottom line is, I think it's a magical and uplifting place for our characters to arrive at the end of their long saga ...[68]

Whether audiences would have embraced *The Shawshank Redemption* without its troublesome final vision of Zihuatanejo is something we will never know. Certainly there is little in the extraordinary history of this film to suggest that critics (or 'purists') understand its charms any better than the members of the public who made it a milestone movie. That final image leaves me frustrated and irritated; others are uplifted. But we are all ultimately enchanted, both by the inexplicable magic of popular cinema, and by the unresolved mystery of Rita Hayworth and *The Shawshank Redemption.*

3 Freeman, from unpublished transcripts for *Shawshank: The Redeeming Feature*.

9 Darabont, 'Screenplay of *The Shawshank Redemption*', p. 105.

0 Robbins, interviewed in *Viewfinder*.

1 Darabont, 'Screenplay of *The Shawshank Redemption*', p. 110.

2 King, *Rita Hayworth and Shawshank Redemption*, p. 83.

3 Darabont, 'Mutatis Mutandis', p. 154. Darabont subsequently e-mailed me to say: With a good deal of time now passed, the dream sequence ... now strikes me as a little too "tricksy" for the film ... part of me feels it is just as well I never had the chance to film

4 Darabont, 'Screenplay of *The Shawshank Redemption*', p. 111.

5 Freeman, from unpublished transcripts for *Shawshank: The Redeeming Feature*.

6 King, *Rita Hayworth and Shawshank Redemption*, p. 110.

57 Ibid., p. 113.

58 Darabont, interviewed in *Shawshank: The Redeeming Feature*.

59 Niki Marvin, interviewed in *Shawshank: The Redeeming Feature*.

60 Liz Glotzer, interviewed in *Shawshank: The Redeeming Feature*.

61 Darabont, 'Mutatis Mutandis', p. 157.

62 Darabont, 'Screenplay of *The Shawshank Redemption*', p. 118.

63 Darabont, 'Mutatis Mutandis', p. 157.

64 Darabont, interviewed in *Shawshank: The Redeeming Feature*.

65 Robbins, interviewed in *Viewfinder*.

66 Freeman, from unpublished transcripts for *Shawshank: The Redeeming Feature*.

67 Glotzer, interviewed in *Shawshank: The Redeeming Feature*.

68 Darabont, 'Mutatis Mutandis', pp. 157–8.

Notes

1 Stephen King, 'Rita Hayworth and the Darabont Redemption', in Frank Darabont, *The Shawshank Redemption: The Shooting Script* (New York: Newmarket Press, 1995), p. xi.
2 Ibid., p. x.
3 Ibid.
4 David J. Schow, interviewed in *Shawshank: The Redeeming Feature* (Andrew Abbott, Channel Four/Noblesgate, 2001).
5 King, 'Rita Hayworth and the Darabont Redemption', p. xii.
6 Ibid.
7 Morgan Freeman, from unpublished transcripts for *Shawshank: The Redeeming Feature*.
8 Stephen King, *Rita Hayworth and Shawshank Redemption*, in *Different Seasons* (1982) (London: Warner Books, 1995), p. 12.
9 Frank Darabont, 'Mutatis Mutandis', in *The Shawshank Redemption: The Shooting Script* (New York: Newmarket Press, 1995), p. 136.
10 Jan Demyan, interviewed in *Shawshank: The Redeeming Feature*.
11 Darabont, 'Mutatis Mutandis', p. 136.
12 Ibid., p. 137.
13 Frank Darabont, 'Screenplay of The Shawshank Redemption', in *The Shawshank Redemption: The Shooting Script* (New York: Newmarket Press, 1995), p. 11 (deleted line).
14 King, *Rita Hayworth and Shawshank Redemption*, p. 29.
15 Ibid., p. 30.
16 Ibid., p. 29.
17 Ibid., p. 30.
18 Ibid., p. 31.
19 Darabont, 'Mutatis Mutandis', p. 142.
20 Tim Robbins, interviewed by Mark Kermode in *Viewfinder*, FilmFour, 2003.

21 Darabont, 'Mutatis Mutandis', p. 141.
22 King, *Rita Hayworth and Shawshank Redemption*, p. 25.
23 Frank Darabont, interviewed in *Shawshank: The Redeeming Feature*.
24 King, *Rita Hayworth and Shawshank Redemption*, p. 24.
25 Ibid., p. 47.
26 Ibid., p. 48.
27 Ibid., p. 37.
28 Darabont, 'Mutatis Mutandis',
29 Darabont, 'Screenplay of The Shawshank Redemption', pp. 62–3.
30 Darabont, 'Mutatis Mutandis',
31 Darabont, 'Screenplay of The Shawshank Redemption', p. 39.
32 King, *Rita Hayworth and Shawshank Redemption*, p. 46.
33 Ibid., p. 59.
34 Ibid., p. 57.
35 Darabont, 'Screenplay of The Shawshank Redemption', p. 13.
36 King, *Rita Hayworth and Shawshank Redemption*, p. 104.
37 King, 'Afterword', in *Different Seasons* (London: Warner Books, 1995),
38 Darabont, 'Screenplay of The Shawshank Redemption', p. 67.
39 King, *Rita Hayworth and Shawshank Redemption*, p. 57.
40 Ibid., p. 23.
41 Ibid., p. 19.
42 Robbins, interviewed in *Viewfinder*
43 King, *Rita Hayworth and Shawshank Redemption*, p. 82.
44 Ibid., p. 56.
45 Ibid., p. 91.
46 Darabont, 'Screenplay of The Shawshank Redemption', p. 99.
47 Darabont, 'Mutatis Mutandis'

Key Make-up Artist
Kevin Haney
Make-up Artists
Monty Westmore
Jeni Lee Dinkel
Key Hairstylist
Phillip Ivey
Hairstylists
Roy Bryson
Pamela Priest
Titles and Opticals
Pacific Title
Colour Timer
David Orr
Music by
Thomas Newman
Music Orchestrator
Thomas Pasatieri
Music Preparation
Julian Bratolyubov
Music Contractor
Leslie Morris
Music Scoring Mixer
Dennis Sands
Music Editor
Bill Bernstein
Assistant Music Editor
James C. Makiej
Music Consultant
Arlene Fishbach Enterprises
Soundtrack
'If I Didn't Care' by Jack
Lawrence, perfomed by The
[Ink Spots]; 'Put the Blame
on Mame' by Allan Roberts,
Doris Fisher; 'Lovesick
Blues' by Cliff Friend, Irving
Mills, performed by Hank
Williams; 'Willie and the
Hand Jive' by Johnny Otis,
performed by The Johnny
Otis Show; *The Marriage of
Figaro* ('Duettino sull'aria')
by Wolfgang Amadeus

Mozart, performed by
Deutsche Oper Berlin,
conducted by Karl Böhm
Production Sound Mixer
Willie Burton
Boom Operator
Marvin Lewis
Cable Person
Kevin Boyd
Post-production Sound
Bald Eagle Sound, Inc
Re-recording Mixers
Robert J. Litt
Elliot Tyson
Michael Herbick
Mixing Recordists
Jack Keller
David Behle
Supervising Sound Editor
John M. Stacy
Sound Editors
Bill Manger
Jeff Clark
Zack Davis
Dale Johnston
Larry Lester
Bruce Bell
Richard Oswald
Assistant Sound Editors
Lori Martino
Bill Weinman
Janelle Showalter
Negative Cutter
D. Bassett & Associates
ADR
Supervisor:
Petra Bach
Recordist:
Rick Canelli
Additional Recordists:
Michael Cerone
Mike Boudry
Mixer:
Tom O'Connell

Additional Mixers:
Paul Zydel
Doc Kane
Editors:
Robert Ulrich
Shelley Rae Hinton
Foley
Artists:
Kevin Bartnof
Ellen Heuer
Recordist:
Ron Grafton
Mixer:
Marilyn Graf
**Transportation
Co-ordinator**
David Marder
Transportation Captain
Fred Culbertson
Drivers
Chick Elwell
Ray Greene
Mickey Guinn
Chuck Ramsey
David Turner
Chip Vincent
William Culbertson
Douglas Miller
Ken Nevin Jr
Scott Ruetenik
Harold Garnsey
Dick Furr
David Smith
Ronald Hogle
Judith Reed
Glen Murphy
James Graham
Tom Park
J. D. Thomas
Robert Conrad
William Davis
Sally Givens
Neil Knoff
Roland Maurer

Gary Mishey
Donald Snyder
Craft Services
Mark Moelter
Don Speakman
Brian Boggs
First Aid
Frank McKeon
Caterer
Joe Schultz
Carlos Garcia
José Lopez
In Memory of
Allen Greene
Stunt Co-ordinator
Jerry Gatlin
Stunt Players
Tom Morga
Ben Scott
Dan Barringer
Mickey Guinn
Dick Hancock
Allen Michael Lerner
Fred Culbertson
Lighting Stand-ins
Dexter Hammett
Max Gerber
David Gilby
Tim Amstutz
Bill Martin
Jon Stinehour
Animal Trainer
Scott Hart
Additional Animal Wrangler
Therese Amadio
Helicopter Pilot
Robert 'Bobby Z' Zajonc
Unit Publicist
Ernie Malik
Publicity
Nancy Seltzer & Associates, Inc

Rita Hayworth Poster Photographed by
Bob Landry, Life Magazine
©Time Warner
Licensed by Princess
Yasmin Aga Khan Jeffries
Marilyn Monroe Poster Photographed by
Sam Shaw, Shaw
Photograph Collection
Licensed by The Estate of Marilyn Monroe
Raquel Welch Poster Photographed by
Hammer Film Productions Limited
Licensed by Raquel Welch
Archie Comic Book
TM&©1993 Archie Comic Publications, Inc
Gilda **(1946) Clip**
Courtesy of Columbia Pictures
Production Equipment
Hollywood Rental Company
Gyrosphere Aerial Camera System
Preston Cinema Systems
Arriflex Camera & Lenses
Joe Dunton & Company International, Inc
Production Dailies Processing
Du Art Film Laboratories, Inc
Dailies Projection System
Boston Light & Sound, Inc
Completion Guaranty Provided through
International Film Guarantors, Inc

Travel Services Provided by
Direct Travel of California, Inc
Photographic Equipment by
Arriflex
Recording Facilities
Warner Hollywood
We Wish to Thank
Dennis Baker, Warden of the Mansfield Correctional Institution;
Richard Hall, Assistant to the Warden;
Manny Centeno, Director of the US Virgin Islands Film Commission;
Eve Lapolla, Ohio Film Commission;
Lee Tasseff, Mansfield Convention & Visitors' Bureau;
The People of Mansfield, Ohio, and Richland County
Special Thanks to
Stephen King

Cast
Tim Robbins
Andy Dufresne
Morgan Freeman
Ellis Boyd 'Red' Redding
Bob Gunton
Warden Samuel Norton
William Sadler
Heywood
Clancy Brown
Captain Myron Hadley
Gil Bellows
Tommy Williams
Mark Rolston
Bogs Diamond

Jeffrey DeMunn
1946 DA
Larry Brandenburg
Skeet
Brian Libby
Floyd
Neil Giuntoli
Jigger
David Proval
Snooze
Joseph Ragno
Ernie
Paul McCrane
Guard Trout
Jude Ciccolella
Guard Mert
James Whitmore
Brooks Hatlen
Renee Blaine
Andy Dufresne's wife
Scott Mann
Glenn Quentin
John Horton
1946 judge
Gordon C. Greene
1947 parole hearings man
Alfonso Freeman
fresh fish con
V. J. Foster
hungry fish con
John E. Summers
new fish guard
Frank Medrano
Fat Ass
Mack Miles
Tyrell
Alan R. Kessler
Laundry Bob
Morgan Lund
Laundry-truck driver
Cornell Wallace
Laundry Leonard

Gary Lee Davis
Rooster
Neil Summers
Pete
Ned Bellamy
Guard Youngblood
Joseph Pecoraro
projectionist
Harold E. Cope Jr
hole guard
Brian Delate
Guard Dekins
Don R. McManus
Guard Wiley
Donald E. Zinn
Moresby Batter
Dorothy Silver
1954 landlady
Robert Haley
1954 Food-Way manager
Dana Snyder
1954 Food-Way woman
John D. Craig
1957 parole hearings man
Ken Magee
Ned Grimes
Eugene C. DePasquale
mail caller
Bill Bolender
Elmo Blatch
Ron Newell
elderly hole guard
John R. Woodward
bullhorn tower guard
Chuck Brauchler
man missing guard
Dion Anderson
Head Bull Haig
Claire Slemmer
bank teller
James Kisicki
bank manager
Rohn Thomas
Bugle editor

Charlie Kearns
1966 DA
Rob Reider
duty guard
Brian Brophy
1967 parole hearings man
Paul Kennedy
1967 Food-Way manager

12,812 feet
142 minutes 22 seconds

Dolby Digital
Colour/Prints by
Technicolor

MPAA: 33087
Filmed on location in Ohio
and the US Virgin Islands

Credits compiled by Markku
Salmi, BFI Filmographic
Unit

Also Published

BFI Modern Classics combine careful research with high-quality writing about contemporary cinema.

If you would like to receive further information about future **BFI Modern Classics** or about other books from BFI Publishing, please fill in your name and address and return this card to us.*

(No stamp required if posted in the UK, Channel Islands, or Isle of Man.)

NAME

ADDRESS

POSTCODE

WHICH **BFI MODERN CLASSIC** DID YOU BUY?

* In USA and Canada, please return your card to:
University of California Press, 2120 Berkeley Way,
Berkeley, CA 94720 USA

BFI Publishing
21 Stephen Street
FREEPOST 7
LONDON
W1E 4AN